# How to Get Along with People in the Church

## A. DONALD BELL

ZONDERVAN PUBLISHING HOUSE

GRAND RAPIDS      MICHIGAN

Third printing    January 1970
Fourth printing   August 1970

*Printed in the United States of America*

*To my mother and father who, by example,
taught me my first lessons in human relations
and
to my wife who skillfully practices these
lessons every day.*

# CONTENTS

# 1. A NEEDED EMPHASIS

# A NEEDED EMPHASIS

## CHAPTER ONE

## A NEEDED EMPHASIS

*Thomas Quinn was failing in his church work. He
knew he was failing. But why? He was dedicated,
trained, and energetic. Why was he ineffective in
church leadership after all these years?*

Although we have more and better trained workers
today, their preparation is usually incomplete. Our church-
related, vocational leaders have been taught in college, university and seminary the Biblical knowledge and organizational methods they need. Our volunteer people have been
well trained by planned programs in the vast laboratory
which a typical church affords. Yet both groups of workers
often fail at Christ's task.

What causes this ineffectiveness? It is at the point of
getting along with the people! In a study made at Carnegie
Technological Institute it was found that ninety per cent
of all working people who fail in their life's vocation fail
because they cannot get along with people.[1] A percentage,
almost as high perhaps, no doubt exists among church
workers who do not succeed at the task.

Most of us need to develop and improve the fine art
of dealing with people. After all, our knowledge of the
Gospel, new educational methods, and all we have to offer
will be limited if we can't reach people in an acceptable
way. Many of us have developed "the art of putting our
feet in our mouths"! Many pastors, ministers of education

[1]Les Giblin, *How to Have Confidence and Power in Dealing With People* (New York: Prentice-Hall, Inc., 1956), p. 4.

and music, superintendents, teachers and training workers fail because they either offend or "browbeat" people.

Where can we find help? There are three main sources: The examples of Christ as He dealt with people; the principles of applied psychology; and the psychology of salesmanship. In the following pages these three source areas are discussed and applications to the role and function of the church worker are made.

### How Christ Dealt with People

The imperfect church worker must study techniques of working with people and yet attempt to use them without being overly conscious of their operation. Whereas Jesus knew the characteristics and the life needs of people by divine power, we must study people by investigation of background or face to face evaluation. This, obviously, is our handicap. Yet, even as in the case of the Master, a deep compassionate love for people will help where skill and wisdom are lacking. We shall see later that our evaluation of people by these methods will determine what techniques we shall use in approaching them. Likewise, Jesus dealt with individuals on the basis of what He knew about them. For example, He justified an embarrassed woman. This was when He complimented the woman who washed His feet with tears, dried them with her hair, and anointed them with precious oil. He did this before the sophisticated guests in the house of Simon, the Pharisee (Luke 7:36-50).

Another time Jesus won a despised man with a compliment when He called to Zacchaeus, "Zacchaeus, make haste, and come down; for today I must abide at thy house." Christ used an almost shocking approach of kindness to deal with a man who never received kindness. He was a publican or *telonai* and was repeatedly linked with the sinner in Christ's day. This was brought on the publicans by themselves and they were stereotyped with all sinners and despised persons. Their practices were such that people hated them as "crooked politicians." They collected taxes from the Jews for the Roman Empire and needless to say abuses dominated. Extortion and bribery were considered "acceptable." Zacchaeus had Jericho as his "tax beat" and never heard a kind word from any Jew. Jesus won him over with this very instrument (Luke 19:1-10).

Again, Jesus asked for something in dealing with a woman who was elevated by His request. This was the instance of His asking for water of the Samaritan woman at Jacob's well. This approach for leading her led to a deep searching of her soul. It would have been expected that she, a Samaritan woman, would have asked Him, a Jew, for something. Jesus frequently surprised people by "turning the tables" and leading them to His way. As with others, He began with her where her life and interests were. Jesus always faced up to the facts of life — He never led people to be evasive. He faced her lowest levels of life socially, morally and emotionally. He went so far, in His facing of issues, as to even say, "Call thy husband." Perhaps we, without Christ's divine license, would tread a little softer, yet often, no doubt, we fail by not being more frank and challenging (John 4:1-30).

On another occasion Jesus intentionally went below the intellectual level of a man in dealing with him. With Nicodemus the Saviour went below the ruler's ecclesiastical and judiciary levels to reach the rock bottom of his simple spiritual needs. Probably Nicodemus would have liked to have led the Master out on tangents of theological discussion, but he could not. Much of Jesus' personal charm was His remaining in the realm of the pure and simple. Some people are not attractive to others because they lack this. Christ never got bogged down in the complexities of doing. He constantly, by simple methods, satisfied the needs of men's lives (John 3:1-14).

Finally, Christ dealt with one person in particular by letting him decide. In the case of the rich young ruler He led him to see the facts, but neither coerced nor persuaded. At other times He went just so far with people and then left them on their own. With some people in certain circumstances that method is, no doubt, the best (Luke 18: 18-26).

These techniques of Jesus and those which have developed out of the experiences of people through the years have yielded certain rules of human relations. These principles when consciously used in dealing with people constitute a part of the field of "applied psychology." We shall look briefly at this second source now.

## The Principles of Applied Psychology

The field of psychology, which is a study of human behavior, has in recent years emphasized the practical and applied aspects of that behavior. That is, many of the leading psychologists have found out proven rules about the way people behave and have made applications of these rules to everyday life. Much of the material in applied psychology has been in the field of human prediction. This means that after exhaustive studies have shown how most people behave under certain circumstances, then psychologists have told us how to deal with people under these circumstances.

For example, applied psychologists have found that most people respond to suggestion better than to force or to argumentation. Dr. George W. Crane in his popular book, *Psychology Applied,* suggests that the average person is very suggestible and the real basis for this goes back to man's instincts and habitual neural patterns. He also suggests that "sales resistance" and inhibiting ideas are not so likely to be set off by suggestion as they are by direct stimulation.[2] The point here is that direct stimulation or coercion may arouse contrary ideas. Most of us have already learned this rule through our own experiences.

The above illustrates how a proven rule in psychology is applied to the field of leading people. Psychologists have

[2]George W. Crane, *Psychology Applied* (Chicago: Hopkins Syndicate, Inc., 1952).

also learned, for example, that there is a difference between rewards and bribes, and much help has been given to leaders in dealing with their followers in this area. Even in the field of church work there is often the tendency to use artificial bribes and rewards instead of genuine satisfactions coming from Christian service. Finally, for example, the social psychologist has found out much about how people behave in groups. We can learn from these findings some ways and means to use the influence of the group in getting the individual to do what we think he should do in the church. Psychologists also have given help on how the individual can influence the total group. In fact, the whole field of social psychology is one that is helpful to any kind of church worker. A typical leader cannot profitably work with enough different kinds of people under sufficiently different circumstances to formulate his own rules of human behavior, and so the leader takes advantage of the years of study and research of applied psychologists in this field of human behavior. A wealth of this material is being written in our day, and the wise church worker is the one who reads current and popular materials as well as some more serious textbooks in the field. In a later chapter we will study a subject from the field of applied psychology which is called "stereotyping."

All of us actually apply psychology in the ways in which we deal with people, though we have not learned specific techniques from psychologists and their works. We have learned some simple rules as we have dealt with people in our own experience. For example, a worker with young people who is not challenging them learns by her own experiences before long that she is not using good "psychology." By repeated poor responses to this approach she learns that it is better to set high standards and expectancy for young people. A wise superintendent can develop a rule of psychology when he learns that scolding a general assembly for poor Sunday school attendance does not improve attendance. He finds out that challenging and encouraging and using suggestion rather than rebuke is usually a better tool.

## The Field of Salesmanship

In recent years the field of psychology and the field of business have merged their resources and developed what we often call the psychology of salesmanship. Since selling is not just an aspect of the business world, but is involved in government, teaching and education, and since human beings do the "buying" in these areas, psychologists have been helpful. Just as the advertiser uses the right approach to reach a certain customer with his product, so must the Christian worker both understand the psychology of his prospective customer and the relationship to his product. His product may be the Gospel itself, a better way of life, more faithful church attendance, a new building program, or any other aspect of the Christian life that he is trying to sell.

Most every community library will have some recent books on the psychology of salesmanship. These will be helpful to the leader or teacher in the church. He only needs to apply the selling experience of the business world to the church situation. For example, if he studies the lists of qualifications for salesmen (out of professional books on salesmanship) he will come to a common list something like this:

*A good salesman will have had personal experience with his own product.* That is, he knows the product and is first sold on it himself before he attempts to present it to a customer. One does not present Christ to others until he has accepted Him himself.

*He will employ honesty in the sales process.* A good salesman is thoroughly honest. He presents both sides of the qualifications of his product, but, of course, emphasizes the better side. He is not just interested in a quick sale but is concerned about continued good relationships with the customer. So it is with a Christian presenting the Gospel.

*He loves his work.* A good salesman does not sell just to make money, but he has a feeling his product can be a help to those who use it. Therefore, he has a genuine sense of industry and enthusiasm in the process. This is essential to good Christian witnessing and leading.

*The salesman himself is significant in the selling process.* His personal appearance and personality are consistent with the type of product he is selling, the customer he is selling it to, and the specific approach he is making in selling. Thus we find the type of salesman selling tombstones is different from the salesman who is selling recordings of popular music. The salesman of a commercial product as well as the Christian worker selling the Gospel is concerned about his role, his physical make-up, his dress, his position, his title, and other aspects that make up the customer's evaluation of him.

*A salesman is a trademark.* Finally, most sales experts would agree that a salesman represents his whole company and industry as well as himself. This means that he is a symbol of more than just his own life and therefore he is a symbol of his product. So the Christian leader represents the entire cause of Christ. Regardless of the type person he is, he has this larger responsibility.

## God Uses All Types of People

We have seen that Christian leaders have these three sources of help: the examples of Christ, the principles of applied psychology, and the psychology of salesmanship. Yet they are still imperfect, sinful people. It must be remembered that through the ages men have marveled at God's method of using all kinds of imperfect human beings to do His will. In His divine and omnipotent power, He could have created some creatures — neither men nor angels — who could have gone forth presenting the Gospel to the world. But, in God's wisdom and economy, He uses the instrumentality of human beings for the evangelization of the world and the care of His people. Men must reach men.

Part of the art of working with and dealing with people

is understanding people. Therefore, each person — a typical human being — is better able to understand and reach another human being. The human aspect of the personality of Christ brought men closer to God. Therefore, God, even today, uses the human element to bring divine wisdom to mankind.

*All persons are imperfect.* On first assumption it would seem that God would select the more perfect of human beings to reach and deal with those who need His message. We find this at variance with His basic plan. God, through the ages, has been able to take imperfect lives and through the regeneration of the Holy Spirit give them spiritual resources which are so powerful that their human imperfections are minimized. Many times people whom the world thinks insufficient are those who, with God's power, are best able to reach others. This fact is not so remarkable when the church worker realizes that those who are to be reached are also imperfect human beings.

Take the example of Bill Smith. He was a fine Christian worker in the First Church of Centerville. Brother Smith, however, was a quiet and modest person. His pastor and other leaders in the church marveled at how much he was able to do for the Lord in his quiet, introverted way. At times of visitation and during recruitment and witnessing for revival meetings, Bill Smith was not able to reach many people. He didn't seem to have that "get up and go" that most of the visitors thought was necessary.

However, those who observed Bill carefully noticed that one day he brought to a meeting a person in the community who had never been inside the church before. His name was Marshall Jones and he was a quiet, reserved but prominent man in the community. Every time someone from the church had tried to reach him, he was unresponsive and the more enthusiasm and pressure utilized, the less response Mr. Jones made. However, it is interesting to note that Bill Smith, who was quiet and reserved, was the only person who was able to meet and reach Marshall Jones. Often in Christian service it seems that a person of one type is better able to meet another person of the same type.

Every Christian worker needs to realize that there are certain people whom he cannot reach and deal with. This is true even of a good pastor of a church. Many times he must turn over a prospect to some lay person who "speaks the language" of the one to be reached.

*Some one person can best reach another.* This is part of the genius of Christ's Church. It means that for every person, regardless of the type of personality he is, there is someone in the community who can best be reached and dealt with by him. The very God who made us all different wants us to continue to be somewhat different. Although most of us could stand some improvement, God does not — upon conversion — change us all into the same kind of creatures. Although we are changed spiritually, most of us remain the same kind of personality generally.

God uses people in different lines of work and different stations of life. All of this is part of His divine plan. In Ephesians 4:7-13, we find these words: "But unto every one of us is given grace according to the measure of the gift of Christ. Wherefore he saith, When he ascended up on high, he led captivity captive, and gave gifts unto men. (Now that he ascended, what is it but that he also descended first into the lower parts of the earth? He that descended is the same also that ascended up far above all heavens, that he might fill all things.) And he gave some, apostles; and some, prophets; and some, evangelists; and some, pastors and teachers; for the perfecting of the saints, for the work of the ministry, for the edifying of the body of Christ: Till we all come in the unity of the faith, and of the knowledge of the Son of God, unto a perfect man, unto the measure of the stature of the fulness of Christ."

The writer of Ephesians could say in our day that in working with people for kingdom causes, Jesus calls men to be businessmen, doctors, farmers, salesmen, teachers, musicians, craftsmen and shopkeepers.

*Individuals are not to lose their identity.* We are living in a day and age when we are pressured on every hand to change ourselves and become what our society expects us to be. We force our children into molds. We constantly talk about the well-rounded man, the well-balanced person. Many of us so disperse our lives in various areas of interest that we lose our personal identity. The irony is that if all of us became this well-rounded American man, life would probably be boring because we would all be just alike.

This means that for the Christian, self-improvement is not necessarily growth toward one particular type of personality in life. Christ wants us to keep some of our identity. Certainly it is evident in the New Testament that we are all to live as though we could achieve the moral and spiritual pattern of the life of Christ. It is not to be inferred, however, that in so doing we would change our entire personalities and characteristics to the extent that we would lose our individuality. The fact of the matter is, one of the most attractive things about human beings is their uniqueness. No two persons are the same physically, emotionally, socially, or in any other way. It is because of the uniqueness of each individual that Christ uses us each in certain tasks to reach certain people for Him.

In the thirteenth verse above we read, "Till we all come in the unity of the faith." This phrase has great psychological meaning for the church leader of our day. It means that, as has been said, he can retain his identity and uniqueness and still be a part of the group called the church. It is wonderful that in joining the fellowship and membership of the church we do not have to lose our personal identity in the group situation. We do, however, come into the unity of the faith.

*Individual differences ought to be retained.* Loss of identity has been, however, the chief requirement for membership in the totalitarian states and groups of history. All of the dictators and tyrants have required that the members of the group lose personal identity. Under Nazism, Socialism, Communism, this is essential. In the work of the church, one can be quiet, reserved Bill Smith or he can be an active, aggressive extroverted William Wilson. One person can serve by working behind the scenes while another can stand on the platform and lead the groups in directed leadership.

Christ uses tens of thousands of Christians who hesitate to speak publicly, but who can write Sunday school lessons, commentaries and books on the Christian life. Christ uses one man on the assembly line to reach another man on the assembly line. He uses a woman who can, over the back fence of her house, reach another woman whom even the pastor could not enlist.

*Christians are a team of specialists.* Therefore the workers of the church, both church-related staff leaders and the lay members, are all specialist members of a team. Everyone, psychologically, is a specialist in Christian service. This can be said because everyone can have a specific responsibility and can do it better than anyone else. Until the Christian understands this stewardship aspect of life, he can never be spiritually or psychologically satisfied. When one sees this stewardship role, and achieves what he can in the situation wherein he finds himself, then he is really able to do the most for Christ and His Church.

Frustrated church workers are those who are always trying to change themselves into that which is expected of them. Happy and successful Christian workers are those who seek to change themselves in that they become more like Christ and yet retain their own talents, abilities and personalities, channeling them into Christian work.

When a salesman has not had many sales and he becomes discouraged in his work, he often reminds himself of the fact that some place in town there is a person who will respond to his sales appeal — one who will like him, understand him and buy his product. He realizes that because of his own individuality, he is better able to show this prospective customer the life need which his product can meet.

So it is with the leader in the church. He may feel that he is untrained, lacking in abilities and rather meek and mild in working with people. From a stewardship standpoint, however, there are in the church community, in the town or in the world, people to whom he can best channel Christ's blessings. There is always something about him and his approach that can successfully bring the Gospel to meet the needs of certain types of people.

*A place of service for everyone.* This leads us to evaluate the various positions which Christians fill on this team of specialists. As in any other enterprises, carried on by human beings, some people will always play certain roles. The aptitudes, talents, experiences and training of some make it best for them to stand in the foreground and work with the larger groups. The experience of others makes it wise for them to be involved in policy making. The abilities of some afford them the wonderful opportunity of working "behind the scenes" and yet seeing the outward results of their work.

The first thing a new Christian must do before he can be used in Christ's service is to evaluate fairly his life, see where he can improve by training in the church's program, and then find his place of service within the structure of the church. As with any other team, no position is unimportant. In many athletic games undue attention is focused on those who carry the ball. But it must always be remembered that without those who block and tackle and sit on the bench as coaches there could be no game.

We live in a day when unless a man is in the swivel chair, upon the pedestal or behind the footlights, it is felt that he is not succeeding. This is a false and materialistic concept. In most cases, the great leaders of the Christian movement have been those who really worked behind the scenes. A worker should never feel that certain positions which are admired by most people are necessarily the places in which he can best serve and work.

Let us look at some examples: The Reverend William S. Johnson had been pastor for a number of years. He had made the necessary sacrifices to train himself in both college and seminary. He had three relatively successful pastorates when an offer came to work with one of the denominational boards. He was not sure of the Lord's will in the matter, and prolonged his decision. Finally, he felt impressed that he ought to take the denominational position. He did so and stayed in it for almost two years.

It soon became evident that he was not well adapted to that type of work and at the end of the period, he was called to a church much larger and with more responsibility than his last pastorate. In that situation he was able to do more than he had ever done before in any church. He had been led into a sojourn with the denominational office. It did something for him that no other experience could have done. However, he now knew for sure that his role of service was in the pastorate.

Mrs. Ruby King had been working for almost twenty-five years with one of the elementary groups in her church. During the week, she was a director of the kindergarten in the local public school. Her experience in working with children was known throughout the city. One day, however, she decided that maybe she needed some variety in her service. Since she worked with children all week long and at the church, too, she asked the nominating committee to consider her for one of the positions with the young people of the church.

After one Sunday in the new situation, she found that she could not deal with young people. She constantly addressed them as "children" and treated them in that way. Before the week was up, she asked the nominating committee to revoke their decision. Soon she was happy working again with her children. She had found where she could best serve and where the Lord wanted her to serve.

Thomas Strong was one of the most successful bookkeepers and accountants in his town. For many years he had served in this vocation and had always felt happy and comfortable in his work. When he was approached to accept an office of the church, he accepted it because it was the superintendency of the Sunday school. He thought that would be a most honorable position in which to serve and that there would be some wonderful privileges in it. He was not egotistical nor materialistic as he viewed the job, but at the same time he did not think of his personal aptitudes, interests and personality.

After he had served for a few weeks as superintendent of the Sunday school, it became obvious to him and others that this was not the place where the Lord wanted him to be. At his own wish and the suggestion of the nominating committee of the church, he was elected to be the treasurer of the church. In this role he felt very much at home. He was adapted to it, he had abilities in the area, he was trained in it, and that is where the Lord could use him best. He worked for many years as the efficient and happy treasurer of that church.

*Some conclusions.* In summary, we can draw several conclusions.

The task of winning the world to Christ is so broad and the people to be reached and dealt with so varied, that Christ uses every type of personality to do the job.

Christian churches need a great team of specialists. These people are specialists in that although they are imperfect human beings, they have natural and learned abilities which have come out of life experiences. With the power of the Holy Spirit, the church member looks at himself, seeks the Lord's will, and responds to the call of the responsible parties of the local church. He finds his place of service.

There is a specific place of service for every Christian somewhere in kingdom enterprises. Because we are human beings and we sometimes misread God's will, it is not unusual for people to get in a temporary position of Christian service. Such sojourns can be remedied by further self analysis, prayer and seeking God's will. Then a careful study of other possibilities and positions of service will help. Because of the fact that no two people are alike, there are some positions which are better than others.

As we think about our stewardship role in reaching others, we are impressed with the fact that God wants us to use the abilities, aptitudes and talents which He gave us. He does in another sense want us to be different. He wants us to be different from the world. Our talents and abilities can only be used after they have been given to Christ. We can find our psychological role in kingdom enterprises only when we have properly positionized ourselves in regeneration. We do become new creatures. God will not necessarily change all the characteristics of our personalities, but they will be henceforth used by Him in a new way.

The tasks are difficult, for we go forth as spiritual salesmen and many of those who need what we have are most difficult to reach. The competition is keen because the competitor, Satan, is more skilled at the task than we are. But we have a product, the Gospel, which can perfectly meet the needs of all. And we have a divine Power and enthusiasm which can penetrate the darkest doubts. We have the advantage and our cause and our Christ will prevail. Be not ashamed of the Gospel of Christ as you deal with people.

Live so as to not be ashamed before God — and you'll not be ashamed before men.

# 2. THE ROLE OF LEADER

# THE ROLE OF LEADER

### THE LEADERSHIP OF JESUS
### DEFINING THE LEADER'S ROLE

## CHAPTER TWO

# THE ROLE OF LEADER

God reveals His Word through the words and acts of men. In Old Testament days God used prophets, wise men, sages and others. Jesus called and trained a rather small group of leaders and relied upon them, with the power of the Holy Spirit, to present His Gospel to the world.

## THE LEADERSHIP OF JESUS

It is interesting that in the brief ministry of Jesus, He did not spend the precious hours seeking to enlist and train as many workers as possible; rather He used a small group of those whom He had chosen and trained. These people were definitely leaders. Since that time God has called certain people to be leaders in kingdom enterprises. Even today a minority of vocational workers and lay people shoulder most of the responsibility of the churches.

*Jesus and His leaders.* The followers of Jesus became the leaders of men. Every Christian worker can profit by interpreting the ways in which Jesus worked with people. Immeasurable value can come from a study of the gospels with emphasis upon His interviews. Insights into human relations are clarified by Jesus' actions. It is evident that He was not shackled with conscious leadership techniques, but rather the divine personality was so full of understanding and love that good methods were the natural outcome.

Jesus was able to select those who — from the raw material of human nature — could become the nucleus of the "soldiers of the cross." At first they were preparing for

29

future leadership in a great enterprise. Jesus knew that if He properly invested in them, after His ascension they would be capable of serving as leaders. Since that time Christ has relied on leadership — both vocational and lay. He has endowed all kinds of imperfect human beings with wonderful talents, improved them with training and called on their devotion. In God's divine wisdom He continues to use human instrumentality.

*Christ's role as leader.* One of the most important things involved in leadership ability is the role one fills as leader. The role is all-inclusive. It includes personality, the symbolism of one's life, position among others, the titles and characteristics of life — in fact, everything about the leader. One's role is constantly changing as people get a different viewpoint of the leader.

Jesus held the perfect role of a leader. He was King of kings, Lord of lords and Leader of leaders. First of all, Christ's role as a leader was divinely established in the miracle of His birth; secondly, He was prepared for leadership because He came from the followship (at least from a human viewpoint). Even today people like a leader who has come from the ranks of the followers. Christ spent most of His life in humble preparation for His brief ministry of leadership. But such investment was as profitable for the Son of God as it is for one today. Thus, Jesus was able to do much in a brief period. As we see this example we find the need for better preparation for the task of our day.

Jesus also followed the role of the good leader in that He paid the price of leadership. This was an expensive price which called for sacrifices. It required constant dedication to the task, for a leader must constantly be on guard or lose his leadership role. Jesus also paid the price of training. He could quote the Scriptures verbatim. He knew the needs and wants of people from both His divine and human experience. Jesus paid the price of loneliness and there were times when, even with His intimate followers,

He knew the distance between Himself and them. He felt the isolation which is characteristic of true leadership.

In addition, Christ had a leadership role in that He was always conscious of His "ambassadorship." There is a kind of symbolism about a leader. He is not just a representative of himself, but of the total cause he represents. This symbolism must be strong and consistent enough that it will be contagious to his secondary leaders. Jesus never left His role. He was the perfect and consistent Image of God. So it is today that Christians are ambassadors of Christ and their role must have the same consistency.

*How Jesus led His leaders.* Christ used two main approaches in dealing with and training the leaders who were to take His Gospel to the ends of the earth. They are mentioned briefly here and discussed in detail later. First He dealt with them by direct methods. One such approach was the use of *praise.* Jesus enlisted His workers by means of the positive; as a rule He did not shame people into responsibilities. He created among His leaders what the psychologist calls good "feeling tone." This means that He dealt with His workers in such a way that they felt good about the cause for which they labored. He was seldom critical nor did He allow dissatisfaction to enter the ranks of the workers. This feeling tone was created chiefly by the very presence of His Being.

Jesus used as a direct method the *compliment.* Some who later, no doubt, became leaders in His work were enlisted by this method. Remember the incident, referred to earlier, of despised Zacchaeus in Luke 19:1-10. Jesus' dealing with the woman who washed His feet with her tears employed the compliment in front of the sophisticated guests in Simon's house (Luke 7:36-50). Again He elevated the Samaritan woman at Jacob's Well and though He dealt with her directly in terms of her sins, the general approach was positive and helpful (John 4:1-30). However, the Saviour was honest and sincere in the use of compliments and never employed them to the artificial extreme of what we now call "soft soap."

The Master seldom used the method of persuasion. There are a few exceptions, but the general approach was *encouragement*. He emphasized stimulation, challenge, enlightment and illustration. When He did persuade, however, He had a right attitude about it and never became argumentative. Christ knew when to stop persuasion. For example, remember again the case of the rich young ruler (Luke 18:18-26). Here Jesus went up to the point of persuasion; having given him the information he needed, He then let him decide. Often Christ went just so far and then left one to take his own action. This "open end" method is often the best one.

Jesus also used some indirect methods of leadership. One of the most effective indirect methods of leadership is that of *conversation*. Jesus was an excellent conversationalist with His followers. The avenues of communication were always kept open between Christ and His secondary leaders. The disciples, no doubt, felt free to discuss with Him whatever task they were about. In our day we find that friction and misunderstanding come when church leaders will not talk out their differences. As a leader of leaders Jesus exemplified communication.

Another indirect method He used was that of simply taking time with His leaders. There are enough incidents in the New Testament to indicate that frequently Christ stepped aside with one or two of His workers and talked to them rather intimately about the task. Many times today church leaders become so involved in the mechanics of the task that they do not take time for real *friendship* with their workers.

Jesus also used the indirect method of *working through His secondary leaders;* that is, He would send them out to do things for Him. Every good leader has learned the art of working through his representatives. Many times the person sent can do the task in a way which cannot be accomplished by the leader.

Finally, Christ used the indirect method of *keeping the confidences of His workers*. They knew that He would back them up in their responsibility once they were selected for it.

### DEFINING THE LEADER'S ROLE

Now that the role and the leadership of Jesus have been discussed as our example, applications must be made to our own situations. One's role as a Christian worker is so all-inclusive and so genuine that he does not "play" his role. Rather, he "is" his role. Church leaders are not acting parts — so we are not talking about "role playing." How can we better understand our own place of service when many times our role of serving is rather vague?

Every church worker could understand his place of service and improve his interpersonal relations with his co-workers if he were to place himself in their positions and look at himself. He would probably find out that he is not exactly what and whom he thinks he is. If he is a training leader, he may learn that his pupils see him as an egotist who tries to know all of the answers. A woman's missionary society president may decide, in such an evaluation, that her followers see her as a dictator. A president of the men's work may find that he is classified as weak and indecisive.

The role in which people see their leader is most important — be it accurate or inaccurate. Their immediate impressions and snap judgments, as well as their sound judgments, determine that role. The wise leader accounts for such viewpoints and in dealing with the followers sets up relationship programs which will, in time, give a better and more concise picture. Socrates said, "Know thyself." Carnegie believed in becoming genuinely interested in others. Christ said, "Love thy neighbor."

Several main characteristics of the leader influence what his workers think of him. Some of them are discussed in the following pages.

*Personality is central.* It is difficult to define personality. One is probably near correct interpretation when he sees it as the total of what he is. This "sum-total" includes more than physical appearance and movement. Many people think that a person who is attractive or different in his physical appearance and who is active and aggressive "has a lot of personality." This is thought, by most psychologists, to be a false concept. No one really has more personality than anyone else. Nor does one have a better personality just because he is more active and *extroverted*. For example, some people in a church feel that a minister of education who is always, seemingly, busy doing things and moving at a rapid pace is always successful. To such people he fits into the role of the "go getter." Yet frequently a worker who functions behind the scenes with a well-developed program may actually be getting more accomplished. However, if the people do not appreciate this, such an *introvert* will probably suffer because his workers see him as passive or lazy.

A church worker must skillfully synchronize what he actually does and what his people think he does. As does any good leader, such a worker must constantly strive for personality improvement and growth in terms of presenting the right role to his people. It is admitted that some temporary leaders purposefully develop themselves into sensational and artificial personalities and gain a temporary following. However, a well balanced (*ambivert*) person usually leads better and longer.

One's role is constantly changing. One's personality is changing, too. Many church workers fail in dealing with people because they do not recognize this fact. A model Sunday school teacher may be seen in one view by her pupils, in another by her fellow teachers, as another personality by the general church membership, and in a different light by the parents of her pupils. As leaders lead, they wisely change these roles to meet needs.

A worker starting a mission church is first in the role

of pioneer. Later he is usually a promoter and builder, and finally, a mature, seasoned administrator. One must be cautioned to still retain continuity in his general personality or such changes would bring poor mental health. They would also bring skepticism in his following. It is a matter of retaining one's identity and personal characteristics and yet being adaptable at the same time. The capable pastor, for example, can be both a flaming evangel on Thursday night and a dignified pastor on Sunday morning. He can also be a personal friend and a good sport at the Monday evening social. A youth leader in a church must be close to her young people and also retain her role as a leader, counselor and mature adult. A degree of skill and flexibility is needed to do that. Such "social distance" is significant.

Finally, it must be emphasized that though role is changing and variable, it is not artificiated to the extent that one loses his genuine character and sincerity. Again we must be reminded, it is not "playing" a role.

*Symbolism is significant.* Dr. Ordway Tead says: "Good administration cannot be impersonal or depersonalized, detached or aloof. The formative, initiating, driving and heartening dynamic of a person at the center of the administrative process is inescapably required. Someone has to give the lead. Someone has to espouse the 'big idea' which is the end in view. Someone has more or less to become the focus or symbol of the 'cause' which is afoot. This does not imply any exploitation of the person of the leader, nor yet any hypnotic building up of power which may mean his exploitation of others. It implies rather a realization of the rightful appeal of direct personal dealings animated by a sensitive feeling of friendly concern. . . . What is generally true in affairs of church, political activities, education, military life, and elsewhere — namely, that people look to personal leaders for the tangible focusing of their loyalty to the institution — is at present in industry and government substantially ignored and denied in practice."[1]

[1]Ordway Tead, *The Art of Administration* (New York: McGraw-Hill Book Co., Inc., 1951), p. 139.

Babe Ruth was more than a famous ball player. He was an international symbol of fair play and good sportsmanship. He almost represents the American way of life to some boys. Any leader is a symbol of more than himself to his followers and to others in the fringe of his constituency. Therefore, he is responsible, to a reasonable degree, for all that he represents. A Christian worker is a symbol of his own church, his entire denomination, and all of Christianity to some people. It has been said that the only glimpse of Christ some people get is in the lives of those who represent Him. This principle is expressed in Scripture by Christians being ambassadors for Christ.

Such symbolism isn't matured in a day. It may take years for a church worker's life to become a worthy symbol to his people. If it does, it will probably include these religious and moral characteristics: "consecration, unselfishness, sincerity, high ideas, humility, vision, and faith."[2] Occasionally, one becomes so representative of the best in his work that he may be called such a name as, "Mr. Sunday School." This prestige isn't easy to bring about. Each leader must ask himself, "What symbol or trade-mark do I represent to my co-workers?" What are our church leaders known for?

Another factor in symbolism is that circumstances determine its meaning. A quiet, diligent druggist or shopkeeper may become a symbol of Christian evangelism to a community. Why? Because the man is known to have engaged extensively and continually in soul-winning. These experiences have given him that reputation. If one becomes a symbol of something through dishonest propaganda, it will not be lasting nor will such symbolism be helpful. Only as people are known for what they have really done, is their "trade-mark" genuine.

Symbolism is a ready tool in working with people. It is facile in use and easy to apply. When one's life immedi-

[2]Mary Frances Johnson Preston, *Christian Leadership* (Nashville: Convention Press, 1957), pp. 26-29.

ately stands for something to a group, he is ready to lead. Thus, the experienced Christian worker has a decided advantage if his symbolism is favorable to what he is doing. If a church clerk has done his work faithfully and well for many years, he may explain some aspect of an issue at a business meeting and the people immediately respect his analysis — he uses his reputation or prestige in this way. Later the prestige factor in one's symbolism will be discussed as a tool for leading people.

Symbolism, or what people stand for, has value in relating Christian work to the community. If a person, whose life stands for Christian principles to society, participates in a worthy community project, such a relationship is unconsciously perceived by the people. On the other hand, if such a person participates in an unwholesome activity then he (unwittingly) puts the Christian stamp of approval on the activity. It is like putting a known trade-mark on the wrong product.

Finally, these facts about peoples' symbolism bring to Christian workers a responsibility in terms of Christian stewardship of life. A man is a poor steward if he has done or said things which make his life a symbol which is unworthy of Christ and His cause.

"Let your light so shine before men, that they may see your good works, and glorify your Father which is in heaven" (Matthew 5:16).

*Position plays a part.* One's influence on people is conditioned by his psychological role of personality and the symbol he presents. Also it is regulated by the position he holds. For instance, the moment one becomes a board member of a church, he is positionized in a certain way by the people. Ordination does this for the minister. Before the president of a missionary society is introduced, she has been placed in a role by the group because of the very fact of her position.

Young Christians are sometimes surprised to notice that people react differently to them after they have accepted

Christ as personal Saviour. Psychologically, their social role
has changed. People expect different characteristics in them,
look for new behavior and respond to their leadership in
new ways. Although we know this is desirable, many new
Christians do not account for it. If a person who is one
of the average members of a group is lifted suddenly to a
place of honor or prestige, the members then see him in a
different role, whether he changes in personality or not.

This means that the official position which the church
worker holds may regulate the techniques he will use in
dealing with other workers. It also means that there must
be a degree of "fitting into" what is expected in that position. Some positions naturally call for direct leadership —
the execution of a program. Such action is and always has
been expected. In other church positions it is traditional
to work slowly and indirectly — with utmost tact. Each
worker must study his position in terms of this "role," his
duty and the expectancy of his followers.

*Titles can determine.* This brings us to the study of the
importance of titles. Some workers in their zeal for service
feel that a title is of little importance. It is true that the
labor is of primary importance, yet *that labor can be limited or enriched by* the worker's title. A certain Sunday
school had a small group of Junior level pupils who were
not adjusting well to the total program. It was decided to
create a special session for them before the regular class
period each Sunday morning. However, when it was established, the worker in charge was announced as the "special
teacher." Much stigma immediately became attached to
membership in the group because of that title. The plan
failed.

A large church, with numerous broken homes and much
family strife, called a trained staff member to counsel with
members having problems of emotional and social implica-
tions. However, the staff member was, unfortunately, given
the title of "counselor" of the church. Therefore, when people went to him for help, they were discussed by others

and before long people went to the worker in secret. Later so much artificial shame became attached to his work that it had to be discontinued. Had he come to the staff as an "assistant pastor" he could have carried on his problem solving work successfully. His title made the difference.

A volunteer worker in a church was asked to serve as a church visitor. She accepted and immediately her title "church visitor," was printed in the bulletin. She did well in her work, yet many people whom she visited felt that she came to their homes out of vocational responsibility to her position, and therefore had difficulty in realizing that she really had a personal concern for them. Perhaps a less formal title would have changed this attitude. Church leaders must seriously consider the emotional reactions of followers to certain titles and work out titles of church-related and volunteer workers carefully. A "president" and a "superintendent" may do the same work, but their workers will respond to them differently because of the feeling tones of the two titles.

The following are qualifications of a good title for a church worker:

1. The title must accurately define what the person will be doing as he performs the major responsibilities of the position.

2. The title must be understood, as to the meaning, by the co-workers.

3. The title ought not bring forth negative reactions because of local misunderstandings, prejudices, provincial meanings or regional customs. Certain titles will not be wisely employed in certain areas.

4. The title should be similar to titles of workers doing the same kind of function in other places. For example, if possible, workers everywhere in the same denomination should be able to interpret it.

5. The title of a church worker should have orthodox meaning consistent with New Testament and denomina-

tional connotations. It should express dignity and enlist respect.

6. Such a title must be wisely and tactfully employed, yet the title of a position ought not be misleading, nor should it be a deceitful "cover-up."

7. Titles, particularly those used before a workers' name, should be used with modesty. Most of them are given in honor and ought to be used by others as they refer to a worker. For example, a volunteer church worker does not call an unenlisted member on the telephone and say, "This is Brother Wilbur Johnson." Rather, he will simply say, "This is Wilbur Johnson from First Church." Paralleling this, a pastor probably ought not to say, "This is the Reverend John Miller." He will be wiser to say "This is John Miller, of the church." Also, the best protocol calls for only medical professionals to refer to themselves or members of their families with the title "Doctor."

Churches and workers ought to make titles aids to dealing with people and not hindrances.

*Introductions help or hinder.* Just as the first course of a dinner may regulate the diner's appetite for the meal, so does the right introduction of a worker condition the way in which he will be received by his followers. Pastors, ministers of education, Sunday school superintendents and other leaders should carefully study all known factors and circumstances before presenting a worker in a new position to the congregation or department. Often a worker gets started off "on the wrong foot" because of an introduction which was psychologically wrong, inaccurate or weak. This can happen in the case of a permanent worker (staff or volunteer) as well as in the case of a speaker for a special occasion.

Suppose that a man has moved to a position in a new church and because he has been prominent in another church is soon elected to the board and serves for some time in this capacity. He is relatively well known by the membership of the church, although it is a rather large

congregation. Even though he has not been in this particular church very long, he is elected to be chairman of the
board because of the fact that he has served so prominently
and successfully in other churches in the past. The pastor
and others responsible for his introduction as the new
chairman of the board seek to be tactful and wise in their
presentation of him.

Here are some suggestions which they follow in the
procedure: First, they seek to understand precisely what he
will be doing and where his responsibilities will terminate
as chairman. The conclusions of this study are carefully
discussed with him and with the board.

Second, they study the likes, prejudices and attitudes
of other followers before presenting the new chairman.
Then the introduction can avoid conflicts with the ideas of
the followers. The worker can be introduced so that no
psychological barriers will be unconsciously generated.
Many times unhappy relationships and mistaken ideas harm
the first period of a new worker's service.

Third, they build a readiness and a spirit of expectancy
in the thinking of the co-workers and followers. New workers
and leaders should not be "thrust" at their followers without such preparation. This readiness can be set up by some
of these methods: As soon as the new worker is elected,
formal announcement of the election can be made in the
church bulletin or paper. The statement should indicate
precisely his title, with whom he will be working, and the
details of the position. Too often we take it for granted
that all of our people understand the duties of a position
even so well-known as chairman of the board. By thus
making the appointment or election official in a publication,
the worker immediately has the needed prestige. Indicate
clearly what the qualifications are and emphasize his experience. Then people will anticipate his serving because they
will feel that he is capable of doing a good job. This also
reduces unnecessary tension and exaggeration of the idea
of his having to "prove himself." Plan welcoming activities

such as receptions, proper introductions to groups and other functions. This includes equipment, literature, any expense money, or other tools that will enable him to function more efficiently.

The president of a small college presented in chapel a young woman who was to direct the religious activities for the school. She had graduated from the same college four years ago. During the interim she had received her master's degree in her field and served in a similar capacity for two years. Without considering this, the president presented her to the student body by using her first name, failing to describe her training and experience, and not positionizing her as having faculty status. The students were so confused about her position that it took the woman over three years to straighten out her role in the eyes of her students and faculty members. First impressions are lasting ones.

A middle-aged layman had served his church for twenty years as a faithful, skilled worker with young people. His reputation was excellent in this area of work. Due to business circumstances he moved to another church in a different city. He was enlisted to do similar work, but his department leader did not find out about his experience and reputation. The initial introduction of the layman to the group was the simple statement of his name and of what he would be doing. Consider how that department leader might have improved the worker's role and made his new work more effective had he found out about him and fully presented his background to the followers.

# 3. DETERMINING THE METHODS

# DETERMINING THE METHODS

## CHAPTER THREE

## DETERMINING THE METHODS

As we have discussed the leader's role it has been evident that certain leadership techniques are best for certain people. How does one determine which approaches are best suited to him? How can he most successfully deal with people on the basis of the kind of person he is? Before a leader can know how to deal with his followers, he must take an inventory of himself. This is the needed area, since there is a wealth of help available about the characteristics of the followers. Yet, self-analysis is difficult, as we learned in the previous chapter. However, he can discover what leadership methods are best for him by evaluating the following: The leader should consider responses, the leader understands his stereotype, the leader evaluates his appearance, the leader weighs his enthusiasm, the leader makes his spirit evident, and the leader expresses enthusiasm before the group.

### THE LEADER SHOULD CONSIDER RESPONSES

A worker can evaluate himself by carefully watching his followers. How do they respond to his leadership? In a way, they mirror his life and techniques. If their responses are too serious, then he needs to develop a sense of humor. If they seem to be irritated by him, he may find that he is dictatorial.

Many times such leaders really do not know about their personality difficulties. Often they are not aware of the faulty methods which they habitually use. It is essential to try to see oneself in others as they react to leadership.

## The Leader Understands His Stereotype

Often a worker has slipped into the characteristics which are thought to be signs of his position. These are often exaggerated. The politician wears a black string tie and kisses more babies than is really necessary, and the judge becomes too much of a stilted and reserved person. These caricatured and extreme roles are called "stereotypes." One feels that he must fit into the role expected of that particular task; then he may go too far and become ridiculous in it.

A good leader abides by that which is expected of him without these extremities. He is not eccentric or peculiar, although the fact that he is a leader will cause him at times to act a little differently from his average follower. Actually, his differences ought to be due to the fact that he is setting an example for his workers. He will be, of necessity, somewhat of a model of that to which he wants to lead them, although his role is in some respects more that of an agent or coach. Each successful leader is seeking to bring people much higher than the standard of the leader's own life. His life should be a step in that direction, at least, and certainly not in conflict with the goal.

Giblin gives three secrets for attracting people as: "acceptance, approval, and appreciation."[1] Notice all three are worthy and exemplary.

## The Leader Evaluates His Appearance

It is evident that many of the physical characteristics of the leader cannot be altered by the individual. However, he must see that one can greatly improve his physical appearance, movement and poise. One of the most obvious means of improving appearance is through grooming and dress. It has been said that clothes do not make the man, but they certainly do help.

This discussion will not involve the social advantages in dressing well and in fashion, but rather will be concerned

[1]Les Giblin, *op. cit.*, pp. 59ff.

with proper dress as an aid to total personality presentation of the church leader. The church leader wants to wisely use every possible asset available to present himself in the right way to his followers. Clothing and grooming become possible tools for this purpose.

There are three basic principles which the church worker can use as guides in selecting the proper clothing for each function. They are as follows:

Propriety. The church worker will always want to wear clothing which is conservative enough for his role as an ambassador of Christ, and yet evidence enough style so he will not give an appearance of being behind the times. Some workers are so conservative in their dress that without realizing it they infer to their followers that they are not keeping up, and there is a transfer of ideas by the followers to their work. This would also mean that the leader should hit a good medium of his constituency in terms of the expense and type of clothes which he wears. Such a program for the use of clothes gives his followers the concept that he is mature and stable, yet progressive.

A second basic principle for clothing grows out of the first one, and it is that the worker will not dress in severe fashions. This means that he will steer clear of temporary fads or any unusual kind of dress which will attract undue attention. One might say, then, that usually the church worker does not dress in "high" fashion. It must be remembered that there is a difference between a severe fashion and the quality of one's clothes. One can wear conservative clothes and yet have clothing of the finest quality. The more we can express quality and not extravagance in every aspect of our ministries, the better the role we will present to our people, since quality is related, in people's thinking, to security. The issue of fashion must be considered in the locality in which the worker finds himself, since in some parts of the country fashions change more rapidly than in others. All of these local and provincial conditions will have to be carefully weighed by the church leader as he selects his wardrobe. We would expect the person to wear informal sports clothes at an assembly or encampment in the West, for example. Too, the economic condition of his constituency will also enter into such decisions.

The third basic rule for the dress of the church worker is that of dressing according to the occasion. We could discuss the pros and cons of clerical dress, but it is sufficient to say that most evangelical church groups feel it to be advantageous that the worker uses different kinds of clothing as aids for various speaking occasions. For example, the worker will use conservative clothing when he participates in a worship service, whereas, if he is a sponsor for a children's picnic, he will probably be wise to wear sports clothes which are commensurate with the occasion. Here again the first rule of propriety enters in, as the worker must be careful that he does not go to either extreme of formality or informality as he seeks to adapt his clothing to the specific church occasion. Any person who deals with the public and recognizes the importance of dress, carefully plans his wardrobe so as to have a variety of clothes which will be appropriate for the various types of occasions which he attends. Thus the church worker, particularly the full-time servant, must evaluate his schedule of duties and activities and select his wardrobe on the basis of his needs. Even the volunteer worker will consider his service to the church as he thinks of his wardrobe. It is not that clothing is significant itself, but that it can be an aid to leading people — a tool. The evaluation of appearance will help the leader in making changes, building role and determining methods.

## The Leader Weighs His Enthusiasm

Although the sincere leader in the political world, in salesmanship, or in the court of law, can have a deep sincerity and enthusiasm because he feels that his work is valuable, no one can have the enthusiasm which is available to the church leader. He is dealing with the human element and with life and death matters constantly. No work in all the world is more serious than that of the church. There-fore, the Christian leader will have strong convictions, and a natural enthusiasm which becomes his best method of leading. This is built upon several things.

The leader himself has experienced, first by conversion and second by Christian living, the things he is trying to offer to others. His understanding of this way of life is not theory, but it comes from his own life experiences.

The Christian leader knows that he is in league with God. He has resources and powers which the leader in other realms of life cannot have. The significance of his work — great though the task is — is made possible only because he is in league with unlimited Power.

The Christian leader has a natural enthusiasm and con-viction because he knows that he has the only solution to man's problems. Christ is the only way out. This has a deep psychological significance and gives to the Christian leader a sense of confidence which would otherwise be im-possible.

Finally, the Christian leader knows that the Christian way of life and the means to it which he presents to the people will eventually be victorious. He knows that in the final reckoning God will have His way. Since the leader is in league with God, this realization of ultimate victory has a profound influence on his attitude in all of his work. If every Christian worker would emphasize this fact in his own leadership, he would seldom become discouraged.

Martin Luther, because of convictions such as these, posted his 95 theses on the doors of the Wittenberg Church in spite of overwhelming odds. The emotional appeal of his bold and enthusiastic actions soon had the attention of all Europe. Certainly there must be some merit in the idea that everyone likes to be on the side of the winner.

The church leader who can generate this kind of inter-est and allegiance is usually a successful one. Every worker must weigh his convictions in order to have this expression of spiritual enthusiasm. It is significant to remember also that the religious leader can build enthusiasm to an all-out conclusion. He is in a situation different from that of the salesman who is simply trying to build enthusiasm to the sale of a product or commodity. No matter how worthwhile the product may be, it is not as significant as salvation and eternal life. Therefore, the religious leader can offer the absolute ultimate as a reward for allegiance to his cause. Perhaps that is the reason the sincere church worker finds such deep satisfactions in his work, and his emotional response and enthusiasm never become a rebuke to him.

It has been said that thought plus emotion equals meaning. The church worker should be cautioned here that there are dangerous limits to enthusiasm and emotional appeal, even though they are sincere. These expressions need to be tempered with thought and common sense. For example, the conversion experience itself is arrived at by a combination of both emotion and intellect (or reasoning). In fact, every major decision of life should have a combination of these two elements. Therefore, if the leader is seeking to guide his followers to goals which they find acceptable for them, he will want the element of reasoning to be involved.

### The Leader Makes His Spirit Evident

What are some of the ways wherein the leader can make this spirit and enthusiasm more evident to his followers?

His personal feelings must be genuine and sincere. Any artificiality about spiritual things can always be detected sooner or later.

He should be wise about expressing his enthusiasm. If the highly emotional appeal is a serious means to get people to do practical things, then those people will more likely accept it intelligently. They will not if it is lacking in depth.

Stress of voice, earnestness in description, depth of the program, and conviction in attitude have proved successful — these will help make this enthusiasm more acceptable. In his book, *Psychology Applied,* Dr. George Crane says, "Sometimes only a few degrees of difference in a man's confidence and enthusiasm will change defeat into victory, for the customer subtly feels the mental state of the salesman. Just as enthusiasm is infectious, so doubt and uncertainty likewise are perceived, by the potential clients, with a resulting lack of decision on their part. As in the realm of mental disease, the attitude of the leader may be the basis of success or failure. A conquering mood on his part is more likely to lead to conquest."[2]

### THE LEADER'S ENTHUSIASM BEFORE THE GROUP

When the leader is dealing with a group situation, there are several things he can do to be sufficiently prepared and in spiritual readiness so that such enthusiasm can be gendered. These suggestions will help from both a practical and a spiritual standpoint.

He must live a consistent Christian life. If the leader lives such a life, when he goes before a group on behalf of Christ (be it a congregation, a Sunday school class, or a church committee) the first step in the direction of a genuine zeal and enthusiasm has already been achieved.

He must make personal preparation in prayer and study. Often one feels that he goes before a Sunday school class feeling "cold" or unprepared. Nothing takes from confidence and enthusiasm like this. Therefore, if the speaker is well prepared in terms of things he wants to say and do and in terms of prayer and spiritual devotion, he goes with a confidence that is invaluable.

He should invoke the Holy Spirit before speaking. Perhaps the prayer of invocation — calling upon the guidance of the Holy Spirit — could be used at more meetings than just the Sunday morning worship service. When the speaker feels that he is being prompted and guided by the Spirit, he feels that what he is about to do, though channeled through a human being, will succeed.

[2]George W. Crane, *op. cit.,* p. 236.

He must be "sold on his subject." As has been mentioned earlier, if the speaker has had personal experience with the particular thing that he is trying to get across to his audience, then a natural enthusiasm results. No matter how much one knows about a thing, he is not really as sure of it as he is when he has been involved in it. It would be difficult for a Sunday school superintendent to be enthusiastic about getting his teachers to visit if he had not had extensive experience in personal visitation himself.

He must show a right balance between emotion and intellect. The most contagious enthusiasm results when enough emotion is involved and it is balanced with reasoning and common sense.

He always uses a positive approach. We do not enlist people's interest and activity when we have a negative, pessimistic approach. When a speaker begins without apology and with a happy, optimistic view, half the job has already been accomplished.

Finally, he builds to a decision. When that which he will say has been so well planned that it unfolds before his audience like a beautiful drama and comes to a high climax, then it brings a decision. A leader must be absolutely sure about the decision or conclusion he wants his followers to reach. Then he logically and prayerfully builds toward that decision. It cannot be done rapidly, but is part of an educational process. As this building is done, enthusiasm increases. If he is successful, his hearers will have reached his high peak of enthusiasm.

## The Leader's Role Determines Methods

In summary we can see that the church leader's role regulates his administrative methods. In our study we have already seen that the role of the worker will determine what leadership methods he uses. As we have considered in these first chapters the leader's imperfections, personal identity, specialization, position and title, personality, symbolism, stereotype and physical appearance, we see that all contribute to his role. One's basic temperament, and the personality built on it, will so positionize a person that certain leadership methods are best for him. Some examples of the relationship of the leader and methods are:

—A strong leader with powerful group leadership ability will usually successfully use direct methods as discussed in Chapter Six.

—A reserved, quiet worker who has the genius for leading from behind the scenes will use indirect and more subtle approaches given in Chapter Five.

—One with a radiant, intimate personality leads through friendship and example.

—A leader with a keen, analytic mind may work best through organization, programs and guided experiences.

—Some persons are of such a type that they lead best in direct contact (a message, "pep talk," or interview). Others work best through letters, articles and referral.

—Some persons find that others respond to them best when they are rather formal and objective; others find intimacy and informality suited best to them.

Whatever the person, his Christian responsibility is stewardship of life. He must determine how God can best use him as a leader. Workers vary and methods change, but the same Gospel is presented.

# 4. UNDERSTANDING PEOPLE

# UNDERSTANDING PEOPLE

We Shall Never Understand People We Prejudge

Misjudging Sets up Wrong Techniques

Ten Ways to Understand People

Understanding People by the Art of Listening

## CHAPTER FOUR

## UNDERSTANDING PEOPLE

We have considered the leader in terms of his steward-ship of service, his leadership role, and how he determines his methods. However, he is limited in working with and leading people unless he understands them. Any person feels inadequate at this point, since man seems to understand himself less than anything in his life.

Although the methods of Jesus were briefly observed, human leaders do not have His divine understanding of people. They can never hope to achieve in the knowledge of people as He did. "He that cometh from above is above all: he that is of the earth is earthly, and speaketh of the earth: he that cometh from heaven is above all. . . . The Father loveth the Son, and hath given all things into his hand" (John 3:31, 35).

God calls us to study and show ourselves approved. In Christian leadership this would include our diligently seeking to understand these whom we enlist, win and train.

### WE SHALL NEVER UNDERSTAND PEOPLE WE PREJUDGE

There are two words of Scripture which contain the central truth of volumes of psychology books on the technique of working with people. In Matthew 7:1 we find the words, "Judge not." If Christian workers would abide by this Scriptural admonition, they would have already taken the first step in understanding people.

Mrs. Brown opened the Sunday school class period with prayer. After she had called on the president of the class to make the announcements about the business affairs of the group, she began to teach the lesson. She had just begun when at the rear of the classroom the door opened and a young woman walked in. The class was composed of older intermediate girls, most of whom came from rather fine homes. Many of them were close friends in high school. As soon as the visiting young lady walked into the room, it was evident that she was not a member of the little group to which the class belonged. The teacher continued her lesson, but carefully watched the girl out of the corner of her eye.

Her first impression of the girl was a judgment. The teacher said to herself, "We don't want that girl in this class." The young lady was dressed in a gaudy fashion and she wore entirely too much make-up. As she came in and sat down, it was evident that she was self-conscious. After class and for several weeks the teacher dealt with the girl as though she were a cheap, undesirable person. In this "snap decision," the teacher had grossly misjudged this girl. She realized this two months later when she visited in her home. Then she became well acquainted with the girl's background and found out that the young lady was living in the home of her grandmother since both of her parents were deceased. No one had ever told her what to wear or how to wear make-up. She was not the harsh, coarse person she appeared to be, for deep down inside she had a sweet Christian spirit and beautiful personality. Yet, for two months the teacher had worked with her on the basis of this wrong conception. Only after much damage had already been done was it known that she was really an entirely different type of person.

How many people have you met recently and "sized up" immediately? How many people have you misjudged? Now that you know them better you see that you really didn't know them and you had been leading them in the wrong way.

## MISJUDGING SETS UP WRONG TECHNIQUES

From a technical standpoint, therefore, we can see that every time a worker misjudges someone, he immediately — and almost unconsciously — sets up a pattern of techniques for working with that person. The tragedy is, of course, that the techniques are the wrong ones since they are built upon a wrong evaluation of the person. It becomes rather obvious in this whole study that certain techniques are more adaptable to certain people than are others. Therefore, if we do not know these people as they really are, wrong techniques will be employed. In addition, for the Christian worker, there is a second tragedy in the situation, for in Luke 6:37, the writer says, "Judge not, and ye shall not be judged: condemn not, and ye shall not be condemned: forgive, and ye shall be forgiven." We also read, "Let us not therefore judge one another any more: but judge this rather, that no man put a stumbling block or an occasion to fall in his brother's way" (Romans 14:13). It is not only poor psychology to immediately judge people, but it is also poor Christianity.

Every human personality has many sides to it. Sometimes these are called "dimensions" and other writers refer to the aspects of personality as "facets." That is why one must be patient so as to get a "full picture" of those with whom he deals.

Obviously, the leader cannot ever know all about a person — that is impossible. But in most church situations there is enough time to learn much before action is taken. Leaders must do the best they can.

## TEN WAYS TO UNDERSTAND PEOPLE

What are some ways to find out enough about people to know what leadership methods are best for them? Following are ten suggestions:

*Be open-minded when you first meet a new person.* Try not to say anything to yourself which would immediately classify or designate him as a certain type of person.

There is always the temptation to "pigeon-hole" people and put them in some sort of artificial classification. This is an unfair and unjust practice. The amateur psychologist specializes in such classification.

Withhold an evaluation of the person until more facts about him have become known. This takes patience because we always want to evaluate the other fellow immediately.

*Study any available records the church has on the individual.* These may only include the point record system. However, even Sunday school and worship attendance, promptness, Bible and lesson study, etc., can give a fair, quantitative index to a person. Some churches will have talent sheets, service records and even anecdotal notes (particularly in the case of children of the church).

Some churches have such complete individual records that they favorably compare with the Cumulative Records of most public schools. Many church leaders feel that we should improve in this area, although it is probably indiscreet to keep confidential records in a church office. It must be understood that records are useless (and even dangerous) unless the church leader uses wisdom in evaluating them.

*Make the most of "listening" opportunities.* It is not just what one says, but how and when he says it. This is so significant a means of understanding people that a full discussion is given later in the chapter.

*Another is to consistently think of the person as an individual and try to avoid the temptation of constantly comparing him with others.* Our Saviour exemplifies this virtue. In fact, the whole Christian approach is based upon understanding and appreciation of the individual. On the other hand, the human part of us motivates to compare one with another. Sometimes this can become biased, and if we are really concerned about helping a person, we will think of him as an individual.

The psychologist calls this personalized view of human study the "vertical approach." This means he sees the person on the basis of what he has done with what he has to work with. The "horizontal approach" is comparative. It asks, "How does he compare with others?" A Christian leader will major on the vertical, but must be somewhat comparative.

*Visit in the person's home.* It is interesting that through its history the modern church has always encouraged home visitation as a part of its program. We visit in the homes of prospective people, not just for enlistment purposes or to win them to Christ, but also to understand them better. It is not by chance that the best workers in Sunday school, training and missionary agencies, and age group organizations are those who visit in the homes of their constituency. We learn much about people and their background when we see them in their home environment.

A certain pastor was often complimented because of the fact that his sermons were down to earth and always met the immediate needs of his people. A fellow pastor asked him about his success in this area. He answered that this was his approach: In his visitation he made mental notes of anything said which indicated a need or a problem. He had developed the ability to retain these impressions in his mind without writing them down. Thus, he was always taking in such information during the week in his visitation and in his conferences. Then when he prepared his messages for Sunday, he drew these things out of his mind and "laid them out" along with his Bible, commentary, note papers and other helps. Therefore, the planning of his messages was always conditioned by the needs which he found in listening to his people.

A minister of education used the same procedure to understand his people and to make the programs and activities which he planned applicable to their immediate needs. Sermon planning and program structuring remain alive when they are constantly related to the immediate needs of the people. Workers find these needs in their truest forms when they come directly from the people in visitation.

Thus, we understand people by finding their real life needs. This information leads us to deal with them in right ways and without prejudice or misjudgment. When the leader knows his people he is able to be fair with them in all relationships.

*Avail yourself of every opportunity to see the person behave in many different situations.* The more different types of emotional circumstances in which you can see one behave, the better you will probably understand him. Try to be with the person when he receives good news or when he is in a time of crisis or sorrow. Sometimes we see a whole new person when we observe a friend meeting an emotional crisis. If you can observe the person when he makes decisions, you will understand him better. Both the decisions he makes, and the way in which he makes them, are indicative of what kind of person he really is.

Then it helps if the leader can be with the person when he is in the positions of leader and follower. This is not too difficult a situation to find around a church, because most people find themselves in both situations. In other words, observe the person when he makes a comment in a committee meeting, as well as when he heads a financial drive. When you observe the person as he is a member of a team situation, you see how he gets along with others. As he leads, you understand his individual characteristics.

A good index to the spiritual aspects of one's personality is the way in which he discusses a spiritual problem. If you will observe him when he discusses a doctrine or a Biblical question, you will learn much about that person. If he is open-minded as he discusses spiritual questions, that indicates one thing. If, however, he is always antagonistic and negative, you have another evaluation of him.

*Study the person's friends.* One of the easiest and most effective ways to understand a person better is to observe his companions. Who does he spend his time with? What kind of people are they? What do they talk about and what are they interested in? This will mean that the worker might have to avail himself of the opportunity of seeing this person in different places. In the church he will only be with a select group of friends and this may not give an accurate indication in this area.

*Learn what his interests are.* Someone has said that we can learn more about people by learning about their interests than in almost any other way. Certainly there is a wealth of truth in this idea. One can see how indicative interests are in understanding his own life. Jot down on a slip of paper a list of the things that you have been interested in over the years. Carefully study them: You have a fair evaluation of your whole life. Or one can jot down the things he is interested in at the present time. If this is done objectively and thoroughly, it gives an interesting personality inventory. Therefore, in conversation and discussion with the individual, the worker can learn much about him by studying his interests.

It will be noticed from time to time that the leader of the church is definitely handicapped if he cannot develop a good conversational ability. Many of the methods and plans for working with people depend on simple conversational skills. Here again we find out about people's interests, likes and dislikes by simple conversation with them. However, if we are constantly quizzing them and are over-curious we will defeat the purpose of our sincere interest in them.

*Learn what takes up the person's leisure time.* When we study how persons use their spare time, what their hobbies and recreational interests are, we see them in a new perspective. Sometimes we are surprised at how some people spend their time. This is always a good indication of the real ideals of a person's life. This information is not always easily obtained and the church worker certainly would not get it by subversive means. Here again, simple conversation becomes a good tool in finding out what a person likes to do with his spare time.

*The most significant indication to the understanding of*

*a person is to find out what basically motivates his life.* In other words, if the leader can find out what the worker lives for, and what he believes in, he has located the very center of his personality structure. This means that everything else about him ties into this one over-all motivation. Sometimes this is called the philosophy of life, sometimes it is called the way of life. Most people do not have it formulated too well, but they still live by it.

Occasionally we meet a person who is so involved in one over-all motivation that we get an entirely new concept of the type of person he is. This goal may be a wholesome thing that helps us appreciate him, or it may not be wholesome. Here again, another facet of his personality is known to us. Usually the person does not actually tell the worker what motivates his life, but the worker, by dealing with him over a period of time, soon learns to understand this intangible yet dominating force.

### UNDERSTANDING PEOPLE BY THE ART OF LISTENING

Dick Morris, an active layman, had just been appointed chairman of the nominating committee of his church. The evening came for the first session and Dick, typical of his behavior, walked into the committee session and started talking. Dick Morris continued to talk and dominate the full hour and a half period of the meeting. As he drove home he thought over the many things that he had "told" the members of the committee and felt satisfied with the evening's activities.

In reality Dick Morris had accomplished virtually nothing. He knew no more about the members of his committee than he did before the meeting, because he had not allowed them to express themselves. Each member of the committee had definite ideas about certain positions to be filled, possible candidates and the needs of the church. Mr. Morris went home without any of this helpful information.

In another church, Randall Roberts had just been appointed chairman of the nominating committee. Before he went to the meeting he made a careful study of each member of his committee. He became familiar with the background, experiences and viewpoints of these committee members. Prior to the session he informally prepared a few stimulating questions and comments. At the beginning of the session Roberts presented them concisely to the committee members in a few sentences. From then on, he merely presided and allowed the members of the committee to express themselves during the session.

As his meeting progressed, he was astounded at how much he learned from his committee. The comments of every committee member relative to the duties and tasks of the positions all supplemented each other and gave everyone a full picture. Also, he learned much about the members themselves. He listened to their comments with eagerness. He sought to catch any deeper feelings beyond the words which they spoke. By doing this, he found out that his committee was representative — all of the interests of the church were here. By listening to their questions, comments, criticisms and suggestions he became confident that whatever action they took would be democratic. He also learned that some of the members needed encouragement and he tactfully tried to draw them out so as to get them to express themselves better. He learned that one or two of them would need some encouragement outside of the regular sessions and he planned to give them some of the prepared leaflets about the duties of those officers whom they were to nominate.

As Mr. Roberts drove home from his one and a half hour committee meeting he reminisced and found that he had learned many things in the brief period of the meeting. He had a whole storehouse of information which he had gotten from the expressions of his committee members, and which he could now use in prayerfully leading them to the completion of their task.

The significant difference in the roles of these two leaders was the fact that the first one had not learned the fine art of listening. The second chairman didn't say much, but he was clever enough to use his committee members as sources of information which he and they needed to have.

*Leaders learn by listening.* We live in a world where we mistakenly believe that a true leader is an extreme extrovert who talks all the time and is able to dominate every situation. There is no greater misconception in our times than this one. It is true that most leaders must be able to sway their followers with direction and eloquence. And yet we all know that some of the best leaders in all spheres of life are those who are capable of doing most of their work behind the scenes. The leader who seeks to dominate every situation is cheating himself out of his best source of leadership information. This source is the expression of his followers.

The leader recognizes the attitudes and feelings of his followers by this simple method of listening. He does this by "reading between the lines," by sensing any hostilities, deep feelings or particular attitudes in the questions, comments and criticisms of his followers. It isn't just the words which people use that indicate their deep feelings, but rather the way in which they use these words.

For example, a new elementary worker came to the staff of a large church. She was eager and enthusiastic about her work. She painstakingly worked out an agenda for her teachers' meetings months in advance. She always came to each session for her workers so full of ideas that she took up all the time telling them her plans. This went on for several weeks and she functioned fairly successfully. However, in time she began to run out of ideas, and many of her suggestions were not actually meeting the needs of her workers.

Finally, someone wisely suggested to her that perhaps one of her best sources of creative ideas and plans was the workers themselves. After all, they were the ones who had immediate contact with the children week by week. They were the ones who were sensitive to the children's needs.

Then the elementary worker turned over a new leaf and in her weekly meetings she allowed the workers to express themselves freely. She became sensitive to everything they said and expressed. They brought some of the best suggestions for plans and procedures which had been found.

One of the geniuses of Christian work is the fact that many of our plans and procedures come from the people who are doing the job. When church and denominational leaders come to the place where they feel that they must only use their own ideas they often stray away from the people's needs. Each leader must constantly listen to his followers, for in this way he finds some of his most creative planning. "Everyone loves a good listener."

*The source of good conversation.* One of the best ways in which to develop an understanding of people is by listening to them in conversation. Though most of us spend a good portion of our time in conversation, many of us have never learned the fine art of it. The person who dominates every conversation is one who cheats himself out of some of life's greatest joys and stops up his great resource area. A person who enters a conversation with strangers and immediately dominates leaves that experience drained of his own ideas and still ignorant about the people whom he has just met. One who quietly listens with some degree of participation leaves the group with a new appreciation of his friends and a deeper understanding of them. Leaders are often tempted to dominate because of the feeling that it is expected.

Another weakness of many leaders is the common fault of the misguided focus of attention. This problem works as follows: The speaker focuses his attention on the words he is saying at the time he says them to his listeners. Then when his listeners respond to his statements he is already focusing his attention on what he will say next. This causes the leader to miss entirely the responses of other people. Thus, he is missing the great opportunity for developing conversation and learning about others. This bad habit also makes conversation a one-sided activity. Though it is some-what related to absent-mindedness it is probably more rooted in self-centeredness.

A good leader focuses his attention on what he is saying while he says it, but then immediately shifts his attention to his listener and catches every word and attitude in that listener's responses. In this way he learns. This type of "attentive listener" is the man who is usually popular with his followers. People want our undivided attention. People are hungry for our listening ear. Therefore the art of listening not only becomes a means of gathering information and help, but it actually becomes a tool or instrument for dealing with people. Many of our most capable leaders in the church began their success by first becoming good conversationalists.

*The listening leader as coach.* All of this "permissive" type of leadership places the modern leader more in the role of a coach than a platform orator. As has been suggested, however, there will be times when certain leadership positions require platform skill, although the role of coach is really more significant. All leaders are human, and weak enough to need all of the resources possibly available. A good percentage of such resources comes from the followers themselves.

This means that we want to work behind the scenes. This will be working in the background but not behind their backs. No misconception ought to be found here. You might say it this way: "We need to be wise as serpents — not sly as foxes." Therefore, when we are patient and understanding we will do our best leadership work through our people.

Remember — everyone loves a good listener!

# 5. SOME INDIRECT METHODS OF LEADING

# SOME INDIRECT METHODS OF LEADING

LEAD WITHOUT DEMAND

BE USED OF GOD TO REACH OTHERS

TAKE TIME FOR PEOPLE

DISCOURAGE FALSE PRAISE

BUILD YOUR REPUTATION TO HELP OTHERS

ADMIT YOUR MISTAKES

LEAD BY EMOTIONAL EXPRESSION

CHAPTER FIVE

# SOME INDIRECT METHODS OF LEADING

Perhaps as never before people are resistant to pressures and demands. For the past two decades there have been increasing demands upon everyone. In business, government and social relations we have been coerced and persuaded until psychological blocks have arisen in the minds of most people. This is a time when subtle and indirect methods are best used. Since God has given man the ability to make his own decisions and the wisdom with which to decide, those who work with people need to respect this principle. For example, Dr. Ordway Tead, national authority on leadership, writes, "The central truth is that the individual's fullest use of his best talents is prompted under the conditions which he has helped to determine and which he cherishes because he finds them helpful to his most satisfying self-expression and growth."[1]

## LEAD WITHOUT DEMAND

Instead of trying to force the workers to accept the leader's ideas he can lead them better by building his suggestions "on their ideas." The leader can say "I like your idea there; now let's go a bit further." A good church worker leads people to carry out God's program by stimulating their thinking, not by dictating the program. "For whosoever exalteth himself shall be abased, and he that humbleth himself shall be exalted" (Luke 14:11). It takes a great deal more time to deal with people in this manner, but

[1]Ordway Tead, *op. cit.*, p. 59.

71

true leadership success is when the leader's ideas become the follower's. That is an excellent investment of time.

In his book, *The Psychology of Dealing with People*, Dr. Wendell White gives the following four suggestions for presenting one's ideas indirectly: "By sparing another from feeling inferior, by sharing another's feeling of independence, by affording another the satisfaction of having more or less originated the idea, and by not making another fear that unless he adheres to the idea which he has backed up he will lose prestige."[2]

When people are won over by the slower, but more effective manner, they usually retain that which they have accepted in a more permanent way. For example, "a Sunday school teacher was concerned about a false idea on a certain doctrine held by one of her pupils. The teacher started to force the correct meaning on the pupil, when she thoughtfully changed her plan. Instead she drew the student into the class discussion each Sunday suggesting that she read the Bible on the subject in between the periods. She then emphasized points of question made by the pupil which led to good doctrinal meanings in general. Gradually, after three months, she led the pupil not only to clarify her belief on this one doctrine, but also in the structure of her general doctrinal beliefs. Eventually she was led to change her false idea without being pushed. Her new concept of the Christian life was a personal, creative thing. She had the rightful satisfaction of self-fulfillment and realization."[3]

This indirect approach calls for several things, particularly for the Sunday school worker. Better lesson preparation is required. It means that if the teacher is going to guide the pupil slowly and gradually he will have to look deeper into the more subtle points of the lesson and use

[2]Wendell White, *The Psychology of Dealing with People* (New York: The Macmillan Company, 1946), pp. 3-7.

[3]A. Donald Bell, *Ten Commandments for Dealing with People in the Church* (Muskogee, Okla.: Hoffman Press, 1955).

class discussion to gradually bring his pupils around to good conclusions. The dictatorial and didactic approach does not achieve such an end.

The teacher will have to understand his pupils better, thus knowing the particular avenues through which he can reach them. He will patiently lead them through their misunderstandings of Bible truths and even some misapplications of these truths. He will finally bring them to the place where they themselves accept the right interpretation and application. Involved in this is also a need for personal visitation in the pupil's home. Then the teacher will know more of the aspects of the pupil's personality and thus be able to reach him better.

A third help in dealing with one indirectly is for the pupil to be enrolled in a small class. The larger the group dealt with the more directive the leader must be. The smaller the group the more personal, subtle and indirect he can be.

Two warnings are appropriate in the use of the indirect method of dealing with people. One is that it does not mean we are working behind people's backs, rather we are working behind scenes. It is not a sly or evasive method of dealing with people. It is honest and sincere and yet does not involve force and coercion. The second misconception of this approach is the fact that it is to be used exclusive of other methods. Needless to say, there are still many times, persons and situations when the church worker must boldly come out and frankly state God's will in a matter. There will even be rare and emergency situations where the worker will rebuke people even as Christ did when He ran the moneychangers out of the Temple.

Christ's cause can always use leaders and workers who are humble, sincere and patient. Perhaps leaders too often assume the role of the forceful director.

## Be Used of God to Reach Others

God has placed in the hands of imperfect human beings His perfect plan for life. Christians transmit this Gospel through their relationships with people. Every friendship affords a chance to get across this message. Every contact offers an indirect method or opportunity to speak about the better life in Christ. Therefore, we cannot be selfish or thoughtless about our human relations; but we must remember that, in a sense, God relies upon us to use them for Him. This is another use of indirect methods.

Contacts are stewardship possibilities! We must utilize them with the people in our churches, if we are to help. This utilization involves several things:

*Our work with others is hampered if we cannot get along with people.* As we have seen, some church workers have developed a good knowledge of the Bible and know the best methods of organizational work, yet they are failing because they cannot deal with people tactfully. Their problem is that of human relations. Every Christian has the responsibility of improving his ability to work with others.

Bill was a leader in his church. He was faithful in attendance and in Bible study. He never missed a training course and he knew methods as well as anyone else in the church. Yet a nominating committee had never made Bill the director of his group. Bill wondered why. Almost everyone else knew, however, because every time Bill opened his mouth he put his foot in it. He offended people and simply could not get along with others. His knowledge of church life was ineffective because of his poor personal relations within the church. Bill was actually limiting God's opportunities to work through Him.

Finally Bill went to his pastor for help. The pastor led him to see how God needed him, and then guided him toward a self-improvement program. Before long, he was more considerate of others and he constantly placed himself in the other person's position. His tactfulness increased as did his popularity. Bill's case is only one of many in our churches.

*What we represent to our co-workers may determine our effectiveness.* It was mentioned earlier that every person is a symbol of something to people. Jesus is not only the world's Saviour; He has become the symbol of goodness, love, peace and faithfulness to the world. Each Christian is a symbol of God, His churches, and all of Christendom. What other workers think of us determines how we can work with them. What symbol do we present in the following situations?

*In the worship service.* A Christian ought to represent consistency in his attendance at worship services. His regularity symbolizes the value of worship; and by his attitude in reverence he leads into devotion those who admire him. This may stand for more than the long speeches of other people. Ralph Waldo Emerson said, "What you are shouts so loud that I cannot hear what you say."

*Serving on committees.* Few relationships can be more intimate in the church than those of working together in committees. Some people are symbols of faithfulness to the task at hand. Others stand for democracy and willingness to change. Still others — on nominating committees, for example — will serve behind the scenes that others may lead.

*In visitation.* When a church member visits other members, he ought to represent the best in tactfulness and friendliness. It is easy for the visitor to imply that he is better and more faithful than the one visited. This is dangerous. The visitor must not be the symbol of the "holier than thou" type.

*Leading the group.* All great leaders are examples and figures to their followers. A necessity of good leadership is a regular self-inventory! When our lives represent to our fellow workers that which they admire, our influence is greater. Then we can use our reputation to help others.

It is right to want to make something out of oneself as a Christian. Personal gain is given by God and should be used in an attitude of Christian stewardship. If one is known as a good Christian, he should not boast about it.

*Finally, our relations within the church must be typical of family fellowship.* After all, the church is a spiritual family, and the church members are our brethren. We are prone to forget that the New Testament church was made up of individuals who would do almost anything for one another. So must the members of this family of the church support one another. Do not be afraid to praise and compliment. Remember that when you criticize a member of your church, you are working against yourself!

Dr. Floy M. Barnard writes, "After we have won our friends to Christ, we must remember they need our friendship and prayers more than ever. We should encourage them in daily Christian living and help them to become active in the service of the Lord; and above all lead them to be Christian witnesses, too."[4]

Truly God reaches persons through our lives. Christ said, "Go ye therefore . . ." (Matthew 28:19a).

## Take Time for People

One significant means of indirect leading is simply that of taking time for people. This involves speaking to them and remembering things about them. Many leaders who should attempt to call colleagues by name have difficulty with names. Some suggestions in this area might be helpful:

—A genuine and sincere interest in each new person, as he is met, will help impress names and characteristics.

—Express this interest when you meet a new person.

—Repeat the new friend's name in conversation just after you've been introduced.

—Associate his name with the things you are learning about him.

—Really listen to him when he talks; that is, do not let your mind wander into sizing him up or on some preoccupation.

[4]Floy M. Barnard, *Christian Witnessing* (Nashville: Convention Press, 1959), p. 18ff.

____Drop him a brief written note the next day, welcoming him to your class, department or church. This not only impresses him with your sincerity, but will help you remember him and his name. The practice of writing short notes of appreciation is a quick, economical and effective method. For many years, Dr. John F. Herget was president of William Jewell College in Missouri. He was greatly loved and appreciated. He deserved this fine reputation because he sincerely and tactfully dealt with people. Each morning upon arrival at his office, President Herget would dictate a brief note of appreciation to people who had done things for him on the previous day. Such brief letters were often sent to people he had recently met. These notes — only a few sentences long — were excellent public relations!

Remember one or two things about each person you meet. If a new couple visits the church with a child, the wise worker mentions the child in a complimentary way next time he sees them. If a worker has met a person briefly, but remembers upon a second meeting that he was feeling ill at the initial contact, he should ask the stranger about his health.

The passing mention of one's home town or state will be carefully remembered by a wise church worker. Most people like to have others remember where they are from. One is always complimented to have a person say, "Oh, yes, I remember seeing you last week at the church dinner," particularly when he thought he was not noticed. These and other simple habits make contacts with new people meaningful and worthwhile.

We fail to make the most of our human relations when we hurry through our contacts with people. If we give the impression that we are rushed, then other people will not come to us for help.

A wealthy man works faithfully in one of our churches in the Southwest. He is in such a vocation that his time is worth money. Many times he can make thousands of dollars in an hour. Yet this wonderful Christian will take time to serve any person in the large church of which he is a member. He takes time for everyone and never seems hurried. He explains that he must serve the Lord with his time as well as with his money; he says that he is most happy when he is talking with someone about the work of his church.

Jesus was not too busy for little details, because He knew that these little things make up people's lives. Time spent invested in human lives is the time which pays the best dividends!

## Discourage False Praise

Another means of indirectly leading is through the receiving and giving of compliments. Many leaders falsely feel that if they can draw from their followers praise and compliments at any cost, it will serve them well. We live in a day when praise is often encouraged, is usually exaggerated, and therefore is not truly satisfying. If we live as we ought and serve as we should, few compliments will be received which will not cause genuine satisfaction.

The Bible teaches that our rewards are to be found in our good works and the unsolicited praise we receive from those who work with us. If our deeds have not been good enough to merit rewards without boasting, then there is something wrong with our leadership or our attitude. The wise leader in church life is so busy praising the work of others that he does not have time, in the first place, to "fish for compliments."

False praise consciously given is a deceitful act on the part of the follower. Perhaps it is more deceitful for a leader to receive a compliment which he knows is not the truth and so in accepting it justify it. In society one finds so much dishonesty in compliments that one is tempted to bring the practice over into church life. A Christian ought to be thoroughly sincere in everything he does and if he is wise, he will make his compliments honest.

Many times this is difficult to do because of that which our society expects in the way of compliments and praise.

Yet almost always the leader can find something about his workers which is worthy of praise. He can voice this without dishonestly giving praise where the follower really does not deserve it. As has been mentioned before, the leader is also deceitful when he allows his followers to praise him knowing that he does not merit such compliments. Therefore, where false praise brings about guilt feelings, honest compliments are edifying to the human life.

A good leader is also careful to encourage his followers consistently. Too often he gets busy in his task and only rewards his followers with a word of encouragement on anniversaries or upon their retirement from a given task in the church. On the other hand, no Christian worker should achieve in his service simply to get complimented for it. Every one of us ought to elevate himself by training, dedication and experience so as to better serve rather than to get credit. Sometimes one feels that this whole area is the avenue through which exaggeration becomes dishonesty.

How wonderfully satisfying it is to the Christian worker, when he has worked hard to do a task well, to have his followers genuinely praise him for the work he has done. When he retires at night he can look into the face of God and know that he has at least in some measure deserved the compliments which have been given him. This is beneficial to healthy personality development.

How tragic it is for a man to end the day having received and accepted credit for things done which he knows deep down in his heart he did not do well. Therefore, false praise and compliments are detrimental to the whole spiritual and moral life of the individual worker. Guilt feelings and withdrawal from reality can even come.

## BUILD YOUR REPUTATION TO HELP OTHERS

Wilson Blair is superintendent of the Sunday school of a church in his city. He has spent a lifetime studying the Scriptures. When he hears a young, rather inexperienced, teacher do a fine job of teaching a Bible lesson he compliments and encourages him. He even gives him suggestions for improvement. He uses his reputation to inspire others in Bible study, not as a means of self-elevation.

Too many Christians misconstrue the true meaning of the stewardship of improvement, just as they do the accumulation of wealth. Such accomplishments ought to be used as tools and instruments in dealing with and in reaching people for Christ.

Along with this one ought not to elevate oneself, as a leader, by pushing others down. This method of worldly competition is unbecoming to a Christian leader. He cannot be selfish or thoughtless about human relations.

### Admit Your Mistakes

When you tell your colleagues you are wrong, people will respect you for it, even though it is the style not to admit weaknesses, wrongs or mistakes.

The sick person always thinks he is right. The healthy person is willing and even eager to admit personal limitations. Pupils admire a Sunday school teacher who freely tells the class his lack of knowledge on certain points. One of our nation's greatest theologians often responded to a question, "I don't know." He was respected all the more for this scholarly and fair attitude.

Somehow our knowledge of our imperfections ties Christians together with a common bond before God. For example, one's Bible knowledge is never complete, for all the answers are not there. Much must be taken on faith. Therefore, church workers, above all people, ought not to be self-sufficient. A wise leader admits his lack of knowledge and says to his followers, "Let's find out more about it. . . ."

We may have to "lose an argument in order to win a soul." Christian leaders should have a humble, learning attitude about the task. They must be forceful without being dogmatic. The indirect method of leadership is, therefore, no sign of weakness to the Christian worker.

## LEAD BY EMOTIONAL EXPRESSION

In our earlier study of enthusiasm we discussed how the knowledge of it helped a church leader know how to use it. Now we want to see how emotion (closely related to enthusiasm) is an indirect method of leading.

What is emotion? Emotion, like human personality, is difficult to define psychologically. One of the best and most concise definitions of emotion is simply a "stirred-up condition." This idea of feeling, which is closely related to emotion, is "the experience of a pleasantness or unpleasantness." The most common emotional expressions are happiness, surprise, fear, anger, disgust and contentment. Some psychologists feel that these come from three basic emotions — three innate emotional patterns: fear, anger and love. Other scholars have itemized emotional expressions into long and extensive lists. Although some people do not express their emotions overtly, but keep them pent up inside, most people give evidences of their feelings.

The leader and speaker who is familiar with the standardized emotional expressions — those which most people understand — will use these movements, gestures and facial expressions to portray an emotional idea to his followers. Also, if he is really concerned and involved in the things he is trying to get his followers to do, then he will emote these deep, stirred-up feelings and they will become a part of what we call "enthusiasm." Webster defines enthusiasm as, "To be inspired or possessed by the god, inspired. Divine inspiration or possession. Ecstasy; transport. Ardent zeal or interest; fervor. For instance, an object or cause, of such interest."

Since the emotional expression of one person suggests similar expression to another, the leader can often use his sincere enthusiasm to incite a similar deep feeling in those with whom he works. This contagion of emotion is rather commonplace. When one becomes elated and excited over a situation and tells his workers about it in glowing terms, they are more than likely to feel the same way he does about the situation. From these and other experiences we can formulate the following principles about the use of emotion by a leader.

*Emotional behavior is contagious.* When one person becomes moved, the other people present are likely to do the same.

*Emotional expression becomes part of the transmission of the leader's enthusiasm.* Enthusiasm becomes alive and vital when emotion is involved in it.

*Emotional expression is a part of zeal that ties the leader to his followers.* The Apostle Paul radiated a strong zeal for his work. This definitely linked him closer to those with whom he worked.

*The emotional appeal by the leader is instantaneous.* Many times it is not as permanent as the educational approach, but it can bring people to action in a hurry. For example, the leader in a church situation can persuade his followers to do something which is difficult for them if he is involved enough himself.

*The emotional appeal tends to express itself in action. In fact, it calls for action.* We would like to think that most people behave and decide on the basis of intellect, but actually most of us make our major decisions on the basis of our emotions.

*The emotional appeal enables the followers to release tensions.* Many times guilt feelings and other tensions have been built up and the church leader can offer emotional outlets in terms of service, dedication, consecration and confession.

*An emotional appeal builds loyalties; in fact, loyalty itself is usually built on strong feelings.* Most Christians are loyal to the church because of their deep feelings about Christ rather than because of church membership, or church constitutions.

The leader who gives a reasonable expression to his inner feelings is usually the person who is admired and liked by those who work with him. There are certain merits in controlling one's emotional expression, and yet there is a simple sincerity about a person who has feelings.

An attractive worker is one who speaks with enthusiasm, makes his decisions deliberately, walks briskly, and is completely confident in the thing he is doing. Such characteristics of a leader naturally stem from a basic conviction about his relationship to God. An artificial conviction in this area will take away from sincerity. It is a pleasure to work with someone who is so thoroughly sold on the thing he is doing that it radiates through everything he does. There is nothing less pleasurable in life than to work with people who are disgruntled and dissatisfied with their tasks.

Many prominent figures in history began the road to success by enthusiastically challenging their followers to do what seemed to be the impossible. These followers, had they just used their reasoning, would never have gone along with the leader; but the emotional appeal and the confidence of the leader enabled the task to be completed.

# 6. SOME DIRECT APPROACHES

## SOME DIRECT APPROACHES

PRESENT A PROGRAM OR PROJECT DIRECTLY

DIRECT ADMINISTRATION BY THE PASTOR

DIRECT LEADERSHIP THROUGH ORGANIZATION

SEEK HELP AND ADVICE FOR DIRECTION

LEAD THEM OUT OF A DISAGREEMENT

ENLIST WORKERS TO SERVE

LEAD THROUGH TEACHING AND COUNSELING

CHAPTER SIX

# SOME DIRECT APPROACHES

We have studied some of the more permissive and indirect ways to guide. In most church situations, where we have no hierarchy and most workers are volunteer, the leader must employ these methods. One employs them skillfully only after years of experience.

On the other hand, in Christian leadership there are those times and persons when a direct approach is the best. There is an urgency in much of Christian service which calls for expediency. The evangelistic and missionary zeal must enter into much of the leadership. Then the leader, confident in God's will, is forceful and direct in his "human engineering." He will never, of course, have the confidence of the Saviour who "anticipated all man's basic moral, emotional and mental problems. There is no area of man's life that our Lord did not understand fully and completely. Every single facet of man's personality Jesus understood absolutely."[1]

Generally a good counselor will come to times when he departs from his customary nondirective approach and enters a definite, directive role. This often happens when the counselee decides to solve his problem by doing something which is unchristian and unethical. So the leader must, at times, leave his permissive, indirect methods and assume direction and persuasion.

Even then, he will be tactful and understanding of his

[1]Guy D. Newman, *When God Invaded History* (Grand Rapids: Zondervan, 1958), p. 72.

87

followers. Dr. W. L. Howse writes that in leading, the church worker must, "1. Take a personal interest; 2. Get and give suggestions; 3. Treat people differently; and 4. Make experiences pleasant."[2]

This means he will set a good "feeling tone" for his followers and create a comfortable climate before he uses the more direct methods of leading. For example, suppose the church leader is setting up a new program which he feels he must positively and directly present to his people. Under the particular circumstances, he feels that a more subtle method would not be best. How does he tactfully, yet directly, present it?

### Present a Program or Project Directly

—Compliment the followers and develop a pleasant mood.

—Link yourself to them.

—Use specificity — don't "beat around the bush."

—Strike at fundamental motive bases.

—Keep your approach moving steadily toward its climax.

—Rise to a convincing note as you approach the climax.

—Affirm and reaffirm the program logically.

—Lead the followers to accept it with their hearts.

For example, direct presentation is clearly demonstrated in Paul's defense of himself before the Jewish mob which was attempting to kill him. Although he was both Jew and Roman, Paul skillfully emphasized his Jewish background and training, and also indicated his importance in social rank among the Jews by reference to the high priest: "Men, brethren, and fathers, hear ye my defence which I make now unto you. (And when they heard that he spake in the Hebrew tongue to them, they kept the more silence: and he saith,) I am verily a man which am a Jew, born in Tarsus, a city in Cilicia, yet brought up in this city at the feet of

[2]W. L. Howse, *The Church Staff and Its Work* (Nashville: The Broadman Press, 1959), pp. 130, 131.

Gamaliel, and taught according to the perfect manner of the law of the fathers, and was zealous toward God, as ye all are this day. And I persecuted this way unto the death, binding and delivering into prisons both men and women. As also the high priest doth bear me witness, and all the estate of the elders: from whom also I received letters unto the brethren, and went to Damascus, to bring them which were there bound unto Jerusalem, for to be punished" (Acts 22:1-5).

Thus, Paul positively and forcefully stated his position and program. This direct approach was characteristic of the apostle. He had a kind of "divine egotism" which roused him to speak with conviction and authority. During these times of modern church life one must give God's plan and program to the people without apology and with conviction and challenge. Let us look at the pastor's role first.

### Direct Administration by the Pastor

The modern pastor is as much an administrator as is a business executive or an institutional president. Since one could not imagine a pastorate without these administrative obligations, the field of pastoral leadership (from this administrative and organizational angle) is of great importance today. Every pastor must seek to make himself familiar with leadership techniques. He has been called to a most high place of service — every moment and every ounce of energy is invaluable. If any person ought to be an efficient administrator, it certainly should be a Christian minister. In view of these facts, a brief study of the pastor as administrator may prove helpful.

*The pastor is leader of the whole church.* Due to the trend toward full-time, paid, specialized workers in the local church, many of our pastors have thought of the minister of education as one who relieves the pastor of responsibilities in this field. The same principle follows with the choir director, church secretary and others. Therefore, we need to see the pastor as the administrator of the total church program. He is, in a sense, the "over-all leader" of his church. This will necessitate his having a working knowledge of all aspects of the program of the church. He will be, then, in the fullest sense of the term, a leader.

If he is the pastor of the whole church he will have leadership responsibilities to all his membership. Our leading American authority in this administrative field, Dr. Ordway Tead, defines leadership as the activity of influencing people to cooperate toward a goal which they have come to find desirable.[3] In like manner the pastor must do what a good teacher does — take people where they are and guide them to where they ought to be. If the leader is to guide his followers he must have a clear-cut conception as to where he wants his people to go. In this he must be direct in his leadership. In a church the pastor serves as shepherd, prophet, counselor and guide. In order to properly carry out these offices the good pastor will know when to lead his people directly and how to lead them by indirect methods.

*An administrator of a democracy.* The pastor of a church is definitely the leader of a democratic group. An understanding of the democratic approach to administration will be exceedingly helpful to him. Some have felt that the leader of a dictatorship or of any autocratic system has a difficult task. However, the democratic leader finds his position even more difficult. The leader of a democratic group must not think that the informality of such an organization makes the task less difficult. Actually the opposite situation is true — the pastor must be direct and yet democratic in his techniques. Democratic leadership is difficult for the pastor because: The pastor must prove himself constantly; the democratic pastor is an over-all leader and is personally responsible for everything under his administration; such leadership calls for special training and skill — the pastor must know these skills; the democratic pastor must know his followers because he represents them; he must constantly

[3]Ordway Tead, *op. cit.*

fight personalized, autocratic leadership; he must always keep a step ahead of his followers; he must be spiritually sensitive to the goals and objectives of his group.

Many other reasons could be given for making the role of pastor difficult and complex. He must be a high type of man with natural and spiritual resources and a wealth of experience and training. *A man with less qualifications could be a dictator, but only the best man can be a successful pastor!*

## Direct Leadership Through Organization

The church leader finds that one of his best direct leadership methods is the program of the church. The minister of education leads through the total church organization including general committees. The volunteer worker utilizes the religious educational structure of Sunday school, training, missionary and other agencies. Other church-related vocational workers and lay leaders use the organization which already exists as the leadership tool.

Too often when the church leader feels the need of some new administrative directive or emphasis he immediately sets about some new organization. This is usually unnecessary since a modern, fully developed church program will already have the organizational structure for most any need of promotion.

Then the leader often works directly in organizations by working through his secondary leaders in the agency or department. For example, a wise departmental superintendent works through his program chairman in order to get across some program material or idea to his followers. Every skilled leader is able to work through his colleagues or secondary leaders.

Finally, a good leader leads directly through his organization when he uses bulletins, letters and other literature. A wise leader invests much time and effort in keeping these "lines of communication" open; a letter from a leader to a follower is one of the best direct methods available.

## Seek Help and Advice for Direction

A wise leader uses the direct approach by seeking the help of his fellow workers — particularly in the planning stages of his program. When they have a voice, they make better workers. He will ask for advice because: When he shares with them they assume more responsibility; asking advice pays a tribute to the ability of the workers — they are complimented; they have the opportunity to "let off steam" and release tensions. After this the leader is often able to be directive and they will usually accept his program.

Often the wise church leader goes about getting this help and advice by the means of individual interviews. As he deals with his workers one by one he is better able to present specifics which are of concern to each particular person. When such groundwork is laid previous to the presentation of projects or plans, the followship feels assured that the leader will not "spring things on them." Some church leaders, apparently, have become directive to the point of being unpredictable. Usually a characteristic of such leadership is this lack of preparation of the followship for plans and procedures.

The president of the men's work in a church had an idea for a stewardship training program. He was convinced that his plan would work and he was usually successful with a straightforward, direct approach with his men. However, he was wise enough to first make luncheon appointments with the officers of his group. He sold them on his plans one by one. When the planning meeting came, all were informed, all had already discussed their viewpoints with him, and much groundwork had been covered. The stewardship training program was successfully launched under his direction.

Requesting evaluation, opinion and comments is always a good approach even when the administration cannot use all of the suggestions.

## LEAD THEM OUT OF A DISAGREEMENT

A good leader also seeks help from his constituency when leading them through a conflict. "What one thing causes most disagreements among workers?" This is not easy to answer since difficulties and problems come in clusters. One problem brings on another — and another! Frequently some minor and insignificant issue may begin the conflict, but the trouble which makes it grow is lack of communication. When two or more people refuse to talk about problems, they invite further friction. Breaches between leaders and followers grow wider without attempts toward understanding opposite views. Psychological walls grow higher just as they do in international relations. People do not *always* solve their problems when they sit down and calmly talk them over — but they often open up new doors of possible solutions. When we refuse to talk, we seal our fate!

*Help of a third party.* George Clark was not getting along with his fellow staff member, John Thompson. They knew they had their troubles, but could not see them as they really were, because they had worked close to them for too long. People can be so close to a thing they lose perspective. A psychologist would say that they cease to be "objective."

Clark and Thompson needed to share their problems with an experienced friend. They needed help to "back away" from their differences and see them without their old emotional attachments. A pastor, educational director, or mature friend could do this. The refreshing viewpoint of another person is helpful. Christians ought to share with others in whom they have confidence — those who keep confidences. We ought to really "share one another's burdens."

*The help of God.* This help from a third party is made even more vital when another Person enters the relationship. That Person is God. When seeking takes place in a setting where God is present, disagreements often seem trivial and insignificant.

Such Christian leading might be defined as: "Sharing

with one who is more experienced, more mature, or more skilled the feelings and attitudes related to a situation and with the consciousness of God as a partner."

Karl Stolz in *Pastoral Psychology* says, "The mind is to overflow with the consciousness of God as a partner in our fortunes rather than a Being whose function is to preserve us from adversity or to rescue us from vicissitudes without our cooperation."[4]

*The help of love.* People can usually overcome differences and disagreements when friendships are based on healthy, vibrant love. However, when this foundation is missing, solutions must necessarily be somewhat artificial. Many times this relationship becomes dormant when leader and followers are not living the kind of lives they ought to live. Being the right kind of people and doing the right kind of things feeds a love.

The question rises, "How can such a healthy relationship be revived or continued?" First, the people involved can continually do things together. Just as we have seen that lack of communication in speaking will foster increased disagreements, so will the lack of common activities. Every team should have found the things which they "can" do together and then do them. Second, they must regularly make sacrifices for one another. Even as love for God grows when one does something for Him, so will love for one another grow with giving. Third, both must accept their weaknesses and freely express them.

In conclusion, disagreements are often extremely difficult to resolve; and they usually call for some compromise and giving up on the part of one or all. How can we expect to do this in harmony if Christian love is not available to soothe the wounds?

Conflicts and disagreements can be worked out if leader and followers will talk about them, seek outside help, look for divine guidance, and keep a loving spirit. In addition,

[4]Karl R. Stolz, *Pastoral Psychology* (New York: Abingdon Cokesbury Press, Revised Edition, 1932), p. 245.

they can keep Christ so at the center of every relationship that disagreements are less likely to arise. They can seek to understand the other person's side of the question — he will "hate the person's wrong idea, but not the other person." They can find the solution of the problem in God's work and if help is needed, some other worker will be glad to assist. They can develop a Christian concern for others — many times we disagree because we are too self-centered. They can enjoy the happiness of coming to a solution. It is always wonderful to "make up" after friends have disagreed and come out victoriously. Those who have never disagreed and worked it out have missed a great satisfaction! Often admitting mistakes is part of this process.

*The outcome of disagreements.* In a disagreement there is one conclusion which the leader must impress on the followers. That is that there are only certain alternative outcomes which are possible. One of these is that *one side in the disagreement must be wrong.* Therefore, that person or group, finding the inaccuracy, agrees to take the action suggested by the other side and the leader. A *compromise line of action,* which uses the suggestions of both, can be followed. This means that the leader, in cooperation with the two parties who disagree, works out an eclectic program of action. That is, the best from both sides of the difference are combined into a good pattern of solution. The third possible solution to disagreements is to *branch out on an entirely new line of action.* This is often the best solution when the two parties come to a deadlock. Therefore the leader can develop (with or without their help) an entirely new approach to the solution. This may be an approach which the disagreeing parties may never come upon or it may be one which is an outgrowth of their two ideas. But this solution differs from number two in that the leader formulates it by himself. A possible line of action when nothing else can be worked out is one which is a little more psychologically involved. This is when *no line of action at all* seems possible. There are some problems which simply come to such a state. Therefore, since no action is possible, the only solution to the difference incorporates a complete change of attitudes by the disagreeing parties. As abstract as this sounds, sometimes it is a good solution in such a case. Here the leader becomes firmly directive.

The leader must remember God may first reveal His plans for the church to him and his committees. Then this knowledge is projected to the staff members and finally to the people for their approval. This divine, three level process is weak if the leadership is faulty. What a wonderful responsibility and opportunity to let God channel His blessings through leadership!

*How to cushion criticism.* There may come times—after all else has been attempted — when the leader must criticize one of his followers. Four simple suggestions may be helpful: Always try to begin a criticism with a compliment of that which the worker *has done well*. Never evaluate a worker's service when fellow workers are present — keep the experience personal and confidential. Do not criticize service without telling the worker how to improve — instruct and encourage him in a better way. Close on a positive note such as: "I know you can do it this new way; call on me to help, won't you?"

A great leader must be able to call his workers to account without alienating them.

## Enlist Workers to Serve

One of the most difficult tasks the church leader confronts is that of enlisting workers. It must be undertaken with a positive and direct attitude. How can it be done?

*In seeking workers, avoid any negative approach.* Such techniques as shaming a person into accepting a position or appealing to his sense of duty should certainly be exceptional and a last resort. When Christ enlisted His followers, it will be noticed that He used a dominantly positive approach. One exception to this however, may be when the leader senses the need to mention some of the realistic aspects of the potential position. Many times it is unwise to enlist a person by the method of implying that everything about the position is pleasant. An intelligent human being knows that there will be difficulties in anything that is worthwhile. However, if these negative difficulties are mentioned, the mentioning ought to be done parenthetically.

*Begin the invitation to serve in a position with the statement that the person has been selected for the job after careful consideration.* Such a statement will not be an exaggeration of the facts, since those committees responsible for enlisting church workers should through prayer and study determine those who are best suited for each position. Telling the person selected that these circumstances have prevailed compliments him and breaks down the idea that the leader is seeking to get anyone who will fill the position. There is also the element of selectivity — the person has been selected from several possibilities for the position.

*Give a job description of the position.* This can be done by having in hand some pieces of literature that describe the responsibilities of the particular task. The leader who is doing the enlistment will have these leaflets ready when he goes for the enlistment interview. If the person does not accept, then he will keep them. If the person does make a commitment, he ought to have them ready to give immediately. This plan appears to be much better than giving literature to the workers at some later date. Most denominational headquarters have complete and attractive leaflets relative to the duties and responsibilities of almost any position in church life. A reasonable stock of these should be kept in the church office so that workers who are in enlistment work can use them in this manner.[5]

*Express to the person the idea that it is believed he can do an excellent job in the particular position.* This infers that the backing of leaders will be given to the worker and also that there is confidence in him. Many people hesi-

[5]cf. Wayne E. Oates, Editor, *An Introduction to Pastoral Psychology* (Nashville: Broadman Press, 1959), chapter 8.

tate to assume volunteer positions because they feel inadequate and because they lack security in themselves. If it
can be impressed upon them that others have confidence in
them, this sometimes can be a foundation upon which a
personal confidence is built.

*They should be told that others are depending upon
them.* This ought not to be emphasized to the extent that
the leader pleads with the person to take the situation. For
too long we have pleaded with and shamed people into
volunteer church work. Too often people accept it with a
sigh and enter into it because they have been put into
the corner.

If the person enlisting the worker will be tactful in
the way this point is presented, this danger can be avoided.
Use a statement such as, "Of the people who were considered for the position, it was felt that you would be particularly dependable and that you could do the job in an
excellent way." Such wording does not pit the person
against possible other contenders, but at the same time
elevates him to a position of responsibility.

*At this time in the appeal, a definite statement should
be made that the person should accept the position in order
to serve the Lord and His cause.* In some cases it will be
wise to mention this at the very offset. However, this is
taken for granted in all types of church work. It may be
wise to begin in the manner mentioned above, but about
the middle of the appeal to emphasize this aspect of service
in case the potential worker has not given sufficient thought
to it. After all, all Christian service is dedicated to Christ.
A chief reason for serving in a church position should be
such a motivation.

*Then the leader should emphasize the welfare of the
potential worker's family, community and even the world.*
By following this emphasis, the potential worker does not
feel that if he takes the situation he will be doing it just
to satisfy himself. In this point, the service to others (the

contribution to the community and the impact on the worker's family) should be elaborated on.

*Another emphasis in enlisting workers can be around the rewards which they personally will receive if they accept the situation.* Though basically all church workers are serving the Lord because they do it for Him, there will be, because of their humanity, an element of personal concern involved. Man is basically egotistical. He is to some degree self-centered. If this is properly regulated, it is nothing to be ashamed of since God made man that way.

A Christian should be egotistical in that he is proud of the Gospel which Christ has given to him. Such an egotism can be healthy and builds up confidence. Therefore, if an appeal can be made to the worker, in terms of personal rewards which he will get out of the service, this egotism will be fed in a healthy way. Too many times these rewards of Christian service are expressed in rather vague and abstract terms. Although the leader ought to itemize for the potential worker some of the spiritual and altruistic satisfactions that will come in the joy of serving, he will also specify some immediate human rewards. For example, a statement such as, "In this position you will meet some of the finest people in this town and will have some wonderful opportunities for making excellent warm friendships," will encourage.

*The leader should invite the prospective worker to pray about accepting the position.* Usually it is best to stop the discussion and pray immediately. This will not be used as a means of pressuring the person, of course. However, it clearly positionizes the situation as being a possible call from God. "The effectual fervent prayer of a righteous man availeth much" (James 5:16b). "Therefore to him that knoweth to do good, and doeth it not, to him it is sin" (James 4:17).

*As soon as the person being enlisted seems at all interested in the situation and feels that the Lord is leading him into the acceptance, a spoken commitment should be gotten from him.* There will be times, however, when it will be best for the leader to have the worker think over the opportunity for a day or two. If this is done, the leader must arrange for a specific time and place when the decision will be made. When this does not seem necessary, and the worker seems ready to make a decision, then the leader ought to press for the decision immediately. Many times a person has been almost ready to accept a church job but he was not led to commit himself to it, and by the time he was again approached his attitude had become lukewarm and he would not go ahead with his convictions. Sometimes the leader can add the person's name to a list of those who have accepted — doing this in his presence.

### Lead Through Teaching and Counseling

Out of our earlier discussion of the leader directing through organizations, we come to the study of interpersonal relations. This develops as it should. Those who criticize church organizations forget that such structures really do not exist except as persons function. It all goes back to people. Working directly through organizations, then, really means *working through people.*

Many things which appear to be weaknesses in the organizational scheme of the church are really misunderstandings in human relations. There is always, for example, the danger of misunderstandings between the leader and the follower due to wrong organizational words or terms.

At other times the ends or goals for which the organization has been built have not been clearly understood. Organization is meaningless when ends and means lose their differentiation. Here again the right communication between leaders and followers is the key.

All of this brings us to see that a skillful worker does some of his best direct leading as he immediately relates to people in teaching and in counseling. A minister of education, for example, can present his program directly as he teaches a training course in organization and methods. A pastor leads an officer into a fuller acceptance of responsibility as he deals with the officer in a counseling relationship. A wise departmental superintendent gets across an administrative viewpoint as she leads (through Sunday school organization) a teacher at the Wednesday evening session.

In fact, one cannot separate the functions of teaching and counseling from those of administration. A Christian leader will always have a teaching element in his leadership — an educational point of view. He will also have a human relations (counseling) frame of reference, if his administration is *person-centered*.

The typical organizational structure of a church enables a leader to teach and counsel when such involves pupil needs. The real results then take place. Ray Rozell says, "Few pupils ever learn anything well unless they need it and realize their needs."[6]

In conclusion, it is evident that an acceptable church worker will find times when a direct approach is the best. Even then, however, it is used with tact and Christian love.

[6]Ray Rozell, *Talks on Sunday School Teaching* (Grand Rapids, Michigan: Zondervan Publishing House, 1956), p. 36.

# 7. WORKING WITH PEOPLE IN GROUPS

# WORKING WITH PEOPLE IN GROUPS

The Church Platform and the Group

The Political Platform

The Educational Platform

The Platform of the Microphone and Screen

The Chairman's Platform

What Is Group Work?

The Size of the Church Group

The Values of Group Work in the Church

## Chapter Seven

# WORKING WITH PEOPLE IN GROUPS

In the previous chapters suggestions have been given for dealing with people in the personal relationships of the church. The ensuing chapter will provide assistance for the church worker as he works with people in group situations. The functions of the church leader usually divide themselves into these two areas of work and one cannot minimize either one of them. A church official can neither delete his responsibility to persons as individuals nor can he fail to meet people's needs as they find themselves in groups. Some leaders have emphasized one of these ministries to the exclusion of another.

## The Church Platform and the Group

This means that the wise leader is one who works with his people by constructing his organizational program in the background, and then is able to effectively present it to his public from the platform of the church. Such a platform might be the pulpit, the platform of the Sunday school classroom, the platform of the superintendents, choral directors, dramatic directors and other similar positions.

There was a day when the only platform of the church was the pulpit, but today the expanded program has provided several platforms from which the various aspects of church life can be projected. This modern development of the local church also provided numerous opportunities for the volunteer worker to use his personality and speaking ability to serve as a leader. With the privilege of the use of such church speaking situations by workers comes the responsibility to use every moment of spoken leadership wisely, tactfully and efficiently. This applies in addition to the volunteer worker, to the full-time church-related worker in positions such as pastor, minister of education, age group director and other supervisors. All church leaders are in need of a deeper impression of the value and power of the church platform with its opportunities and possibilities.

The power of any speaking platform is seldom fully understood by the constituency. Christ spent considerable time in His earthly ministry leading individuals and counseling with people as persons. However, His ministries to groups are dominant in His earthly life. Christ had that ability, for which we all must strive, to deal with groups and yet emphasize the individual. Instances like the Sermon on the Mount exemplify Christ's usage of a religious platform for speaking. Since that time it has been impossible to estimate the value of group leadership, through speaking, in kingdom enterprises. Christ's spoken words generated this influence which has come down from generation to generation.

### The Political Platform

Another powerful platform which has been evidenced in history is the platform of diplomacy and politics. For example, a man like William Jennings Bryan was an inconspicuous Congressman from the Midwest, yet his platform ability was such that when he spoke to a group of delegates he was immediately nominated for the presidency of the United States.

Mr. Bryan made this address at the age of only thirty-six years and was so skilled as a platform speaker that his entire life was changed. Exceptional knowledge of political platforms and good government is often unnoticed in a minor political leader because he lacks the ability to properly use his public speaking opportunities. On the other hand, some unscrupulous men, gifted in speaking, have become outstanding political leaders while their legal abilities in this area have been technically weak. A wise church leader will be discreet in his use of this powerful instrument.

## THE EDUCATIONAL PLATFORM

Another prominent and powerful platform is that of education. This one is closer to the church situation. The thousands of school platforms of our nation are utilized five days a week. Many thousands of Christian teachers present their subject matter in ways which are consistent with the Christian views. Since they are speaking from these school platforms to children in their most formative years, no one can estimate the significance of such teaching.

In 1929, Dr. Harry C. Munro wrote a book entitled *The Church, a School*. Then shortly after that he wrote a sequel, *The Church — a School in Christian Living*. With that book and other similar emphasis, the American religious education movement began. A new kind of teaching platform developed. This is the one of religious education which includes the teaching of the Sunday school teacher, the Bible school worker, the leader in the training group, the worker with youth, the teacher of religious education methods, the religious educational teacher in college and seminary, and most denominational leaders. This new teaching platform of religious education has become a great influence in most modern evangelical denominations.

Christ's Gospel ought to be taught to people of all ages by the best educational methods known. This platform is a significant one, and everyone in Christian work must be aware of it. Some of this teaching of Christian truths will be done in individual interviews, but most of it will be done in groups. Such learning groups ought not to be too large. "Sunday school, another common meeting ground between leaders and groups, is a combination of small groups for work and play, with the necessary emphasis on individual action."[1] One who has such a responsibility as

[1]Rudolph M. Whittenberg, *So You Want to Help People, a Mental Hygiene Primer for Group Leaders* (New York: Association Press, 1958), p. 160.

teaching these groups ought to be aware of the best group methods. Therefore, we are going to look at some of the best principles of good group work and are doing so for the benefit of these Christian teachers who teach Christ's Gospel, and its application to human life, to groups both small and large.

## The Platform of the Microphone and the Screen

Another platform for reaching groups has developed in recent years. It is that of radio and television. Though the average lay worker will probably not work through this medium, the specialized and church-related leadership now have many opportunities. The religious speaker in radio now must have enough understanding of group work and sufficient comprehension of his average listener to reach him at his point of interest.

He must also be skilled in making up for the visual aids which usually accompany group work and are significant in it. To some degree, he will have to draw on the emotions of his followers with the inflection, intensity and speed of his speaking since this is the only means of emotional control. Since the listeners in his audience cannot respond, he must anticipate their responses and give a "we" feeling in the total process.

Therefore, radio broadcasting becomes one of the most difficult types of group leadership in all of church life. Many such leaders have developed panel discussions on radio which suggest questions and answers the average listener might have in mind. This definitely increases the group feeling and overcomes the barrier of distance.

In television the religious speaker has the advantage of the visual possibilities. The group feeling is much more easily achieved. Some worship services of local churches, for example, have been so skillfully televised that the viewer at home feels that he is a part of the worship family and is definitely involved in the experience. When the service is poorly projected the viewer feels that he is just "looking in on" the services of some other group of worshipers. Therefore, it is rather obvious that a basic knowledge of group psychology is essential to good religious televising.

## The Chairman's Platform

One of the unique leadership opportunities for all evangelical church workers is that of serving as chairman or moderator of a group. Because of the democratic emphasis in modern life this particular leadership role is essential. There are several brief suggestions which can be given to the moderator in terms of his dealing with groups. All of the principles of good group leadership would apply here since the modern concept of group work is a democratic one.

Some of the functions which the chairman assumes in preparing the group for discussion and business are: See that the seating arrangements and the general fixtures of the room are such as to encourage intense group feeling and activity. "Polarize" the group from the very beginning — get their minds on the item of business at hand which means that the initial remarks of the chairman ought to be well-planned. Build up the prestige of the group so as to prepare them for the exchange of ideas and the assumption of responsibility. Act as a buffer when opposing views are expressed by group members. Understand and execute parliamentary procedure and remain completely democratic in the whole process. Gradually build a feeling of togetherness and participation within the group rather than the debating or argumentative atmosphere. Remain nondirective and permissive in all relationships. Formulate the conclusions and summary in a concise manner, and with the exact meaning unaltered. Conclude the meeting with the assignment of responsibilities and the execution of the action of the total group.

It can be seen from the above that the role of chairman in a democratic, Christian group is not an easy one.

An understanding of the sharing and give and take of groups is virtually essential.

## What Is Group Work?

Group work includes any activities where one or more leaders, in a passive role, lead that group to express itself. It can release desires, show false practices, create healthy anxiety about self, bring out psychological conflicts in personality, and allow one to be influenced by the opinions and experiences of others.

When people get together in groups to do certain business or solve common problems there develops a kind of phenomenon in which the "group mind" develops. It is a kind of experience where, when properly directed, "too many cooks help the broth." People have worked together in groups since ancient times, and grouping seems to be a natural phenomenon in all of nature. There have always been flocks, schools, herds, swarms, masses, crowds, colonies, droves and other groupings.

Even primitive people have always gotten together to solve their problems and initiate new work. Many ancients were acquainted with mob psychology and group control. The ancient Roman teachers were skilled in group teaching and they gathered a circle of disciples around them. Roman diplomats were skilled in this, too, as in the case of Cicero. Christ led individuals in groups and when He spoke to groups His emphasis was always on the individual person within that grouping. Modern schools and Sunday schools use grading as a method of making groups more homogeneous. This approach usually enables common interests and problems to fall within that individual group and therefore work is easy and effective.

A formal and scientific approach to group theory and counseling in the United States first began in the medical field in dealing with victims of physical illnesses. Then the method was used to help groups who were emotionally disturbed or psychotic and later was scientifically used with people who were normal. We in the church are concerned about it in the area of everyday problems and constructive thinking.

Group leadership and principles are now used in many institutions, general hospitals, the military, business and industry, and in the field of recreation.

## THE SIZE OF THE CHURCH GROUP

As has already been seen, there are many church situations in which group leadership and group counseling methods can be used. Thus, the circumstances and particularly the size of such groups will vary. The size of groups can be broken down into a rather specific science. For our purposes, however, we are going to think of four main sizes which also constitute four levels of group work.

*First, the less formal and largest one is the teaching group.* This may be fifty or more people and though the group process is definitely involved, the solving of problems and the exchange that comes from discussion is at a minimum with this size. This type of group work is often referred to as "didactic" and is a simple teaching process with some response and exchange from the members of the group. It takes a skilled teacher to keep this number of people from simply being listeners to a lecture. However, an experienced leader can get the group process working and a degree of discussion, exchange and personality development can take place.

The fact that this large group cannot be seated informally but must usually be seated in rows of seats takes from the effectiveness of the group process. Sometimes, however, this large a group can be seated in a semi-circular form with the speaker in the center and rather close to them. This of course will help. If this large constituency is housed in a room which is just big enough to meet its needs the group process is better than if it meets in too large an auditorium. Informal lighting which is not too bright will also lead to a better oneness in such a situation.

Several "stage materials" can be of benefit here. They are charts, graphs, diagrams and pictures. Having a member of the group participate by coming forward and making a comment about the material discussed is helpful. The use of chalk board, or printed material which is read, is also effective. To break down the "distance" in this large a group the leader must begin by linking himself to his participants in some way. Such intimacy must be genuine and it ought to have to do with his leader's role as a real friend.

*The next smaller group with which the church leader will deal might be called the "discussion group."* It should have between thirty and fifty members in it. This group comes together for a pointed discussion of some problem project. It is not for the purpose so much of solving individual problems as it is for coming to general conclusions by a group with some common interest. For example, a group of about thirty-five young people can be expressive, creative and even developmental in their pooling of ideas around courtship and marriage. Because of the smaller size, this group will have more individual discussion than the teaching group which has just been mentioned. At the same time it is still too large for much individual work by the leader himself.

In other words the discussion group seeks to select and define some common problems and then to develop ideas and insights which will be helpful to all. They are to identify themselves by their comments and questions related to needs in this area. Then under the leader's rather permissive direction helpful resources should be discovered. The over-all planning committee for a money-raising campaign in a church could constitute such a group. After a few meetings the group would divide into smaller and more specialized committees. Therefore, in terms of specific business this size is still a little unwieldy for details.

In leading this second size group the chairman will do certain things. First, he must be prepared beforehand. As in all group situations the leader is a nondirective guide.

He has a general idea of what is to be covered, although he does not predetermine the conclusions of the group. This fact will require that he have some plans for the group experience. Then, he will always remain in control of the situation. He is not in a teaching role as he was in the larger group and so this begins to require considerably more skill.

Also he will serve as the presiding officer, although in most study groups of this type informality is in order. For example, the steps in a group process of from thirty to thirty-five people could be something like this: One, the conference leader calls the meeting to order and a prayer is given. Two, there are general opening remarks by the leader to set the "climate" for the session. Three, the problem to be solved or study to be made is carefully outlined by the leader. Four, the group responds to this and gives some new reactions which may cause a revision of the study area. Five, the members of the group will usually start dividing into various sub-groups depending on their viewpoints. This minor antagonism should be encouraged within limits.

Along the way the leader will see to it that there is a balance of responses and that conclusions will be fair. There will be times when he will have to be particularly tactful in terms of drawing out certain people. At other times he may even have to cope with those who seek to dominate the discussion. Finally, his big task is to give an unbiased summary and conclusion of the functions of the group.

Sometimes this size group will have a panel of from three to eight people to lead the discussion. This will mean that questions can come from the group and the chairman usually directs them to specific members of the panel. The panel discussion is much like a forum, but is more directed because of the resource people, who take the lead. One requirement of the panel discussion is that the personnel of the panel must be qualified in some special ways above the average member of that larger group. This does not always mean that it must be a "panel of experts." It must be remembered that the group is not an audience but rather they participate with the panel. This type is particularly good for church work. For example, the panel might include the pastor and staff of the church as they discuss some question in church life. This could be done in the presence of an interested group from the congregation. It is one way of leadership that definitely is incased in pure democracy.

Sometimes this size group is, as was suggested above, a kind of steering or leading committee for some project which will later be superseded with specially appointed committees. If this is the case the group of this size can frequently have several specialized persons involved in it. This could include, in addition to the leader, a recorder, an observer and a resource person.

For example, if the steering committee is launching a building program for a church, certainly a recorder should be present to make it more businesslike. An observer would be one who gives special attention to what takes place in terms of the clarity of goals, and the participation of the group — that is, how democratic the responses are. The bits of information, the viewpoints that come out of the discussion, and finally any definite conclusions to which the group has come will be evaluated by this observer. The resource person in this type of thing could be a visiting architect, contractor or builder. Incidentally, the chairman of such a group could be a temporary moderator or an interim chairman. He could be pastor, regular chairman of buildings and grounds, or of the building committee. He will have the responsibility of getting the group acquainted with the task and establishing some rules. Then he will give any vital statistics or basic information which the group needs in the proposed planning, and also he will tell what the limitations of the steering committee are. It would also be his responsibility to call on the resource person for clarification and analysis.

*A third size group is the smaller study group for prob-*

*lem solving or program planning.* This group should run from eight to twenty-five people in size. It is the typical working group of the church. This group can be a committee or board and is usually the size group through which the group leader executes most of his work. Some feel that it is the strategic grouping in any democratic organization. The work is really done here. The leader has a little more authority with this size group and yet a church must constantly be aware of the democratic processes. This is also the size group which can get much work done in a short length of time. Much of the background work and interchange which was involved in the larger groups will not consume the time of the smaller groups.

The committee or board should meet in the right kind of room and the church should have a room just designated and furnished for this type of group. A large table with chairs around it is one of the best investments that a church can make in terms of its efficiency in business and programing.

Sometimes this group will take on the characteristics of a seminar, the difference being that in a seminar specifically assigned responsibilities have been accomplished by the members of the group before they come to the meeting. It is more like a study committee or board. Too, the seminar has the idea of research in its activities. It is in a sense the method which we use for the smaller group whose assignment involves coming to a definite decision or bringing specific facts back to the church. Groundwork is essential in this type of function. Often such a study group is called a conference. It meets the same personnel qualifications. "In order to participate intelligently in a conference, the individuals who comprise the group must have knowledge and experience on which to draw, in line with the problem under discussion. This is the basic requirement for any conference."[2]

[2]Alfred M. Cooper, *How to Conduct Conferences* (New York: McGraw-Hill Book Co., Inc., second edition, 1946), p. 136.

The leader of this businesslike group should be aware of certain facts:

Each person should do his own thinking. He has made preparation — he has come to certain conclusions; therefore he should be able to express them.

No important matter should be looked over or passed by. This kind of group needs to have sufficient time to function so that objective results can come forth. The various groups in the church which are represented by these particular group members rely on their voice in the matter. Therefore, the chairman should be sure that the various committee members can express the feelings of their organization or agency. Usually it is better to have fewer, longer sessions.

The leader must keep this type of group function in a definite businesslike atmosphere. It is neither a discussion group nor a social function.

The leader will be sure that the group keeps on the appointed agenda and that all conclusions relate only to this particular area of study.

Sometimes this type and size of group constitutes the "converts class." Many churches have a period of training, usually led by the pastor, for those who have just come into the fellowship of the church. This group — after a revival meeting — offers a wonderful opportunity for leadership. It is a didactic group in that it is a teaching group, yet in terms of size it will resemble the second and third type groups.

Some skilled pastors have also drawn from their individual counseling those people with common problem areas into a group such as this one. This is the right size for good group counseling. When the leader uses this group-counseling approach there are about nine things that he should bear in mind. Let us list these.

—The size of the group ought to be a little smaller than the range indicated above. Probably fifteen is as large as one can successfully handle for emotional and spiritual problems.

__The room and atmosphere should be informal and intimate.

__The more alike in characteristics the members of the group, the better group counseling will take place.

__The more identical the problems of the individuals the better the situation.

__If there is a similarity in age more help will usually come out of the experience.

__The same individuals must attend the sessions consistently. Any turnover in the group process takes from its efficiency.

__Usually one period a week of at least one hour in duration brings the best results in group counseling.

__The leader must be permissive and nondirective.

__Usually the counseling leader in the church will employ the individual counseling method along with the group approach.

*The fourth and final size is the group wherein deep therapy is employed by the leader.* In all cases the group will be less than ten people. Usually we do not have many such situations in a church. However, some of our leadership is skilled enough to perform rather specialized counseling activities. This would be a close group with rather severe emotional problems.

We could liken this group to the situation of the church leader who deals with a few people who are having a definite conflict in terms of working together. These people could be lay-volunteers or staff members of a church. Sometimes there is a rather high emotional content to their problems even though they are not emotionally disturbed.

Many of our specialized church-related workers have opportunity for this type of leadership. They are hospital and penal chaplains, counselors and guidance officials in Christian colleges and schools, trained chaplains in business, industry and the military, and vocationally trained social workers in our good will centers and children's homes.

## The Values of Group Work in the Church

Although they have not thought of their functions as group experiences, most of our church leaders are doing this work in an informal way. After all, the church leader is constantly dealing with groups of all sizes and frequently is employing some of the best psychological techniques without defining them. Such workers can learn much from the leaders we have mentioned earlier — in religion, in politics, in the field of education, radio and television, and also in business and industry. Jesus kept His ministry person-centered even though He dwelt with groups constantly. Therefore the group method is an orthodox technique for a church leader. It is good because it can be supplemented with individual contacts, it saves much time and energy, most problems have a social aspect to them anyway, problems or projects are confronted by all, it allows members to release tensions, it gives confidence to those who participate, it gives the leader opportunity to learn what his people are thinking.

"The human needs for which guidance services are provided are common to all of us. Daily we make choices of some sort — what to wear, what to eat, what to buy, what to do in work or recreation. Often these choices are trivial, but sometimes they are momentous in their influences upon our lives. Decisions about a vocation, choice of a specific job, or a marriage partner, religious or social affiliations are permanent and profound in their effects. Cumulatively, all decisions, big or little play an important part in determining what we are becoming."[3]

[3]Margaret E. Bennett, *Guidance in Groups* (New York: McGraw-Hill Book Co., Inc., 1955), p. 1.

# 8. REACHING THE HARD TO REACH

# REACHING THE HARD TO REACH

The Successful and Wealthy

Those Self-centered People

Timid and Lonely People

The Discouraged and Disgruntled

Our Independent Teen-agers

The Single Adult

Our Aging Senior Citizens

## CHAPTER EIGHT

# REACHING THE HARD TO REACH

Now that we have investigated some indirect and direct ways of working with people, we are going to look at the typical types of people who are hard to deal with. There are always those who are difficult to reach. They may be difficult to reach because of the type persons they are or because of the particular situations in which they find themselves. We are going to try to find some help in leading the successful and wealthy, those self-centered people, the timid and lonely, the discouraged and disgruntled, the independent teen-ager, the single adult and our aging senior citizens. Needless to say, there are no fixed methods which will work in these cases. In addition to listing some typical methods which might be helpful for each, typical case studies will be given which will involve some methods which have proven successful. It will mean then that many times the approaches which are considered psychologically sound for general groups will not wisely apply to these exceptional types.

*One of the basic laws of the field of education has been: take the person where he is and lead him where you want him.* There is no better application in this field of dealing with special or exceptional people, than that one. It means that the leader must be skilled in finding out "where" these people really are. Sometimes in our haste to reach people we fail to take the time to find out where they really are in terms of various levels. This includes their social levels, their religious levels, particularly their interest levels, their economic levels and their motivational levels. If any group of leaders ought to be willing to go where the people really are, it ought to be Christians. Our Saviour was criticized by many of the people of His day because He was courageous enough to do that very thing. For example, "And when they saw it, they all murmured, saying, That he had gone to be guest with a man that is a sinner" (Luke 19:7). Most of the time, in our case, it will be difficult to find out exactly where the person is. Sometimes the skilled psychiatrist has difficulty at this point. We do have some helps, however, and they are drawn from the ten ways to better understand people which were listed earlier in Chapter Four. The ones which are especially helpful here are: Make the most of listening, visit in the person's home and see him under different situations, study his friends and interests, find out how he uses his leisure time, and locate what basically motivates his life.

*Usually the variable in understanding the hard to reach is the individual personality.* It will be noticed in the types that we are discussing in this chapter that some are considered hard to reach because of the particular life situation in which they find themselves or a period of growth through which they are going. Most of them, however, are difficult to reach because of some personality trait which they have. For example, why did one businessman respond to certain life situations by having an exaggerated feeling of success and satisfaction? Why does another person lose himself in "business"? How is it that one person who lives in the midst of an active church community becomes lonesome? On and on it goes and one is immediately confronted with the fact that individual personality differences make the person as he is. A basic knowledge of psychology is helpful at this point. Most church leaders have had many experiences in working with people, both in their general schedule of life and in their specialized leadership positions in the church. Therefore, many leaders will have a good fundamental understanding of human psychology.

*If the leader who is seeking to reach the hard to reach*

*will study the basic life needs of these people, he will find a whole new avenue of approach.* The late Dale Carnegie repeated in all of his writing and speaking his basic principle which was that we lead people to want what we want them to have by understanding their basic needs. He also felt that many people were not conscious of what they really wanted, and that the leader has a sacred stewardship to bring to them the things which are genuinely satisfying to them. Much of the applied psychology of our day is based around the area of human needs. Practically all of the psychology of salesmanship is geared to this same general principle. A wise leader of people will be able to get down to their basic and fundamental life needs and out of them he will pitch his appeals to satisfy those needs. Many of the people who appear to be hard to reach are simply people who have found ways outside the church to satisfy their needs. Many times these ways are not acceptable and it means that the Christian worker must provide the most acceptable and only rewarding satisfactions. These are the Christian solutions.

*Another factor which the leader of these people must consider is that many times life circumstances make them hard to reach.* In the discussion on understanding people the initial suggestion was that we be open-minded and that we withhold an evaluation of individuals. This would be particularly pertinent in considering these people. It means that many of them have built up resistance to the church because of their different ways of satisfying their life needs. The more one understands the circumstantial factors, the more he can appreciate the attempts the individual has made to satisfy his life needs. This will make the Christian worker much more sympathetic and understanding of the person who is difficult to bring into successful service in the kingdom.

*One is enabled to reach the difficult ones by attempting to see their side of the situation.* This is a natural outgrowth of trying to understand their circumstances. Among the Indian tribes of the West there is an old saying, "Walk for three days in thy brother's moccasins before you judge him." Our modern paraphrase of this, "Put yourself in the other fellow's shoes," still embodies some good basic psychology. If we would be successful in leading those who are difficult to lead we must definitely see their point of view.

It will be helpful if the leader will appeal to the following: basic needs, basic interests, the use of new and creative activities, need for security, desire for conformity, desire for influence and prestige, need for wholesome recognition, rights to satisfactions for competency, indispensability and usefulness, and loyalty and friendship.

First, we shall evaluate some ways to reach the successful and the wealthy.

## The Successful and Wealthy

Many times those who are in places of prominence and who have acquired social prestige and wealth are the most difficult to reach for the Lord. This is not to say that such a situation is always true — although some Christian leaders have thought so. It does infer, however, that some of our standard approaches for winning people to Christ or enlisting them for more active service do not work in reaching this particular group. One of the first things that must be considered in reaching these busy people is the fact that their time is extremely valuable. The initial contact with such persons in this category must be well-planned and well-timed. It is not unusual for a Christian worker to have to make a private appointment with one in this group. Sometimes it will have to be in the business office of the individual. If it is a soul-winning interview there may be more appropriate places where one can be introduced to the busy person and where the informality of the occasion might contribute to the possibilities.

If one is trying to reach such a prominent or wealthy person to subscribe to a building campaign or in some other way to contribute time or money to the church, it is often more advantageous to state the purpose of one's call at the time one arranges such an appointment. Wealthy and prominent people are accustomed to being asked for things. This is so frequent in their lives that they do not want the solicitor to "creep up on their blind side." It may be much wiser to let them know why you are coming before the time of the conference.

Then, it is often found that the wealthy or prominent person can be best reached for the church by working through some other person on his level. Frequently the pastor of a typical layman in the church cannot himself reach the prominent or wealthy person. He may try first, but when his approach does not work it is often the best psychology to work through some other successful layman in whom the person to be reached has much confidence. The Christian witness of the prominent and successful people in our churches is therefore strategic. It means that in many cases they are the only ones who can reach lost people of prominence. Our Christian institutions must depend, largely, upon the wealthy people within our ranks to encourage other wealthy people to contribute to our causes. Many people in places of prominence and wealth have been active Christians early in their lives, but the preoccupation with success has estranged them from the church. Therefore, they are not often reached by the typical church leadership but by wealthy Christian colleagues in whom they have confidence in the business and social world. People who are successful take the suggestions of other successful people seriously. If one active and wealthy person calls an inactive wealthy friend and suggests that he become more active in a financial campaign in the church, that person is usually reached. One can say it this way, that the nearer one can "speak the language" of the successful and wealthy person, the better able he is to reach him for any kingdom enterprises.

One of the danger zones in reaching such people is that the approach will infer that they are only being sought for Christ because of the prestige of their names or they are only being approached because of the money they have. Therefore, it means that the Christian witness or solicitor must be wise and tactful as he presents to such persons what the new church relationship can do.

This is evidenced on the modern scene in terms of Christian philanthropy. So many wealthy people have been approached constantly for gifts to church causes that the majority of them have now set up their wealth in foundation funds which are run by boards or committees. This means that the wealthy individual does not even decide himself where his money will be given in terms of charitable and church causes. Many of these prominent and wealthy people have set up such foundations because those of us in the church and welfare work have been neither tactful nor courteous in our approaches to them.

It should not be inferred, however, that this discussion means that the average church leader should shy away from trying to reach people who are members of this group. We need to be impressed with the fact that Christianity is a faith for the up-and-outer as well as for the down-and-outer. Perhaps many of us have failed at the point of wise stewardship here. In other words, when we can win or enlist to more active service a prominent or wealthy person for the church, he in turn usually enlists additional people. Influence is a big thing in all types of Christian service. Therefore, we must see the wonderful opportunities in these privileged people of our church communities and develop new and better means for reaching them. One of the most meaningful Christian witnesses is that of a dedicated man who is successful and wealthy. God can use these achievements to great service in His name.

The above discussion has dealt with some methods of reaching these privileged people. There must be behind any techniques a profound and personal concern for spiritual welfare. All people are souls with the same basic needs. The characteristics of position do not change this fact. Often the successful are lonesome, unhappy, and searching. First must come spiritual concern — then psychological approaches!

## Those Self-Centered People

One of the best psychological definitions of personal maturity is the one which indicates that a human being is mature when he produces more than he takes in. This definition gives the idea of independence and readiness for responsibility. When we apply such a psychological definition to the Christian reference we have a beautiful definition of Christian maturity. This means that a person is mature when he has lived enough, undergone enough problems, and focused his life on what God has already given to him. The immature person is always "self-centered" — the truly mature person is always "others-centered." A mature Christian is not only outgoing in the social welfare sense, but outgoing in bringing the Gospel to others.

One can say it this way. When a Christian is so full and over-flowing with God's blessings to him and he is a mature enough person to realize it, then he will have a compulsion to pass some of these blessings on to others and forget himself. Let us look at the following examples of the causes of self-centeredness.

Judge Philip DuBerry was free from his duties in the court on Tuesday afternoon and decided to spend the time in visitation for the Sunday school department of which he was superintendent. The judge had developed a real interest in two families who were enrolled in the adult department. They would make profitable visiting for the afternoon.

Later, coming home from his two visitation experiences, the judge could not help but compare the two families he had just contacted. The personalities of each couple were opposite. The first couple, the Joneses, lived in a lovely home on Maple Drive. They were a typical couple, yet somehow neither husband nor wife was very mature. They talked about trivial things. They were overly proud of their home and its furnishings. Their entire conversation centered around themselves.

As he drove on the judge could not help but compare them with the Browns, the second family visited. The Browns lived in a similar home and their family situation was comparable. Yet the contrast in their personal maturity was almost startling to the judge. This second couple knew what they were about. They were able to make decisions immediately. They were not only ready but eager to share their Christian experiences with others in the department and also with the unenlisted. Every suggestion made by the judge was quickly taken up and evaluated with maturity. They seldom mentioned themselves at all.

When the judge finally stopped in the driveway of his own home he sat for a while and wondered why there was such a difference in the basic life attitudes of two couples. He had known these young adults for many years. Both couples had their difficulties and trials. Both of them had happy moments and disappointments. Each couple had been blessed with children who basically had about the same aptitudes and abilities. Yet the one couple evidenced no concern for others, a self-centeredness and little maturity. The other couple had certainly achieved these virtues. Then the judge realized again that it isn't the life situations that people undergo which bring real Christian maturity, but rather their individual responses to these life situations.

The judge tried to list for himself some of the things through which these couples had gone and then tried to remember their particular reactions to them. First he thought of the changes. Both couples had certainly had many of them. In fact, who could live in this world without undergoing many changes? But somehow in the case of the first couple these changes (which should have made them altruistic) had only made them more self-centered. In the case of the more mature couple there had been seasoning and a growing sense of responsibility to others. The judge thought how adults could make the most of experiences of change. He felt that the Browns had done a beautiful job in making the most of the opportunities that had faced them year by year.

Then he thought about the problems the two couples had faced. He remembered the financial reversal that the Jones boy had shortly after he was married. It had certainly been a deep valley of despair for both of them. It could have been a wonderful experience, however, and they could have come through anxious to help others in need. But he remembered how they had blamed God and pitied themselves. He then thought about the Browns and how, when their first child was to be born, tragedy stepped in and took the life of the baby. Yet when they faced the issue of God's will, this life problem led them toward sympathy to others. They had been a wonderful example to the other young adults in the church. It seemed that within that one year of their tragedy both Mr. and Mrs. Brown had grown greatly in the understanding of God's will for human life.

In a most interesting translation of the New Testament by Phillips, we find this rendering of verses 14-16 of the fourth chapter of Ephesians: "We are not meant to remain as children at the mercy of every chance wind of teaching and jockeying of them who are expert in the crafty presentation of lies. But we are meant to hold firmly to the truth in love, and to grow up in every way under Christ, the head. For it is from the head that the whole body, as a harmonious structure knit together by the joints with which it is provided, grows by the proper functioning of individual parts to its full maturity." Yes, thought the judge, the Browns had certainly matured in Christlikeness through the problems of their lives.

Christian maturity infers decentralization of self and concern for the lost and needy. In the example given above, it is evident that the Browns were concerned about goals and ideals much larger than themselves, and that the Joneses were all wrapped up in themselves. They could be reached and helped by being led to find more satisfaction in doing, on Christ's behalf, for others than in doing for self. This emphasis is beautifully given in the Scriptural admonition concerning "one of the least of our brethren." A good way to lead people out of self-centeredness is to see that one finds more satisfaction in giving something to others than in getting something for one's self.

All of the characteristics of true Christian maturity have to do with the individual's relationship to God and his contacts with his fellows. The social aspect cannot be minimized. This means that those working in the church have a wonderful opportunity in bringing Christian maturity to self-centered persons. They have the opportunity because they are able to relate people to God and to deal with them in a Christian social environment. The functions and activities of a typical church provide experiences which take from self-centeredness.

In summary, one reaches those self-centered people by leading them to a personal inventory, guiding them to "count their many blessings," showing them the joy and satisfaction of serving others, and bringing them to a fuller dedication of life.

### Timid and Lonely People

It is astounding to realize that in a thickly populated area such as our land, there are hundreds of thousands of people who are timid, provincial and even lonely. Some of the most lonesome people in America are those living in the midst of our bustling cities. Some of the most timid people are those who live in highly socialized villages and towns. Many times these people hesitate to become active in church experiences because of this timidity. Often the person who is lonesome does not want to be that way and only needs help and encouragement to enter into group experiences.

Let us first look at the timid person and try to find some simple helps in reaching him. The first suggestion is to find out the cause of his timidity. This may be easy or difficult — depending on the circumstances. Sometimes the timid person is the one who has some kind of inferiority feeling in his make-up, or it may be that he has feelings of shame or disgrace because of some condition in his personal life or family. Without undue prying or unethical investigation, the person trying to reach such a timid one for the church ought to find out what he can do about the individual's life.

Frequently the best initial approach is to visit the timid one in his own home. Something here may be the cause of his difficulty and the reason for his hesitation to get out and assert himself in the activities of a church family. This being the case, the Christian witness has a divine compulsion to "go out into the highways and hedges and compel." This will be done in a tactful, friendly way, not in an attitude which says, "I have come here to find out what is wrong with you." In such an initial visit the worker may find it wise to simply stop by as a friend, not even persuading the person in terms of church attendance or enlistment. However, anyone doing work for the church will not hide the fact — it will be stated briefly in the initial visit with the timid person.

In dealing with this type, the person trying to reach the timid one can find much help from current writings in the field of counseling.* It may be that in such initial contacts the church visitor will have to draw out the timid person and lead him to talk and tell about his life situation. Sometimes this is difficult, but usually such a person is anxious to share his experiences with someone who is sympathetic, understanding and loving. The timid person is much like a child in that he must be helped in his first steps. In most cases the visitor will arrange to go with him the first time he goes to the church. He will probably sit with him and encourage him in the worship experience. Many times these moments are the most profitable that any church leader can spend.

*One of the best and most recent is Dr. Clyde M. Narramore's *The Psychology of Counseling*, Zondervan, 1960.

Now let us look at the lonesome person. Here again we begin at the point of trying to understand the cause of his lonesomeness. It may be a personality difficulty and we may tactfully want to bring the pastor into our relationship with the lonesome one. Many times such people are those who feel that they are not needed. The task of the church leader is to impress upon the person that he is important in the eyes of Christ and that there is a place of service and a need for him in the gospel plan. If such lonesome people can once get into the fellowship of the church and have their social needs satisfied in a Christian environment, the task is usually successful. Sometimes the method of taking a group of young people to the lonely person's house — particularly if he is an invalid or ill — is employed. This is good if it is genuine and natural, but if it gives the guise of being an artificial method of operation, then it may do more harm than good. By this it is meant that if the invalid feels it is a routine part of the mission program, it will not satisfy his need for genuine friendship.

One of the best mechanical means for enlisting the lonesome person in the church is to take literature on visits. It should tell about the functions of the church, such as bulletins and the local church papers. Many times one has so separated himself from church life that he has literally forgotten the wonderful Christian fellowship that takes place there. As he is reminded about it and reads about it, his need becomes evident and his hunger finds a place of satisfaction. It is probably better, with the lonesome person, to lead him to the place where he wants to find Christian fellowship and steps out on his own to achieve it. This was not necessarily true of the timid person who needed help in the first steps of affiliating himself with the church group. That becomes one of the points of difference in reaching these two different types. Many of the other approaches are common for both.

In conclusion, it must be remembered that one gets into a state of timidity and isolation over a period of time by building up wrong habit patterns. In like manner, it may take some time for a person who is either lonely or timid to get completely out of his state and into normal Christian social relations. Therefore, the education program of the church, through its functions and organizations, can serve beautifully here. The typical active church already has programing which is available to gradually educate introverted people into a happy, normal Christian fellowship.

## THE DISCOURAGED AND DISGRUNTLED

Bill Wilson placed his telephone in its cradle slowly and methodically — a look of dismay was on his face as he recalled the telephone conversation. One of his best workers was discouraged and blue — contemplating resignation.

Mr. Wilson, minister of education at First Church, was concerned about his disgruntled departmental superintendent, Robert Sterling. Mr. Sterling had served for several years and had evidenced disappointment and disillusionment recently. Wilson had to admit that the phone call was not too much of a surprise. He arranged to have lunch the next day with Mr. Sterling and he knew that he must plan his approaches carefully. He felt confident that Sterling's feeling of failure in his task was purely in his mind and that really he was doing an acceptable job as superintendent. How could the education director lead him to see that things would not always go smoothly?

That night as he lay in bed trying to go to sleep, he thought about some of the causes of discouragement that workers like Mr. Sterling experience. He thought of the fact that many of them have motives for their work which are not the best. Perhaps Sterling had originally accepted the position because it would give him an opportunity to express himself to his fellows. He may have accepted it with the desire to gain prestige rather than to serve. It could also be that he first became discouraged when he had failed at some task. Many times the church worker in a new situation fails to understand that everything will not succeed and that some attempts and methods are bound to fail.

Then he thought that there might be clashes between Mr. Sterling's personality and those of his co-workers. Maybe there was friction within his department. There was always the possibility of his not receiving the satisfaction from his work that he ought to have. Perhaps he had expected his teachers to compliment his leadership more and maybe he was hungry for approval. There is always the possibility of a worker not understanding the relationship of his position to the total task of the church. That is, there is often failure in fitting into the organizational scheme. Though Mr. Sterling had an understanding of the religious education program, there would be this possibility.

Just before the good education director drifted off to sleep, he offered a prayer for his endeavors at the luncheon engagement on the next day.

When the two men met for lunch, the education director had some definite ideas of approach all ready. He knew that he must be flexible, but he felt that he had better be prepared. His first determination was to have a positive and enthusiastic attitude as he talked to his discouraged group leader. This had to be genuine and carefully distinguished from a blind optimism which might have been artificial. This initial approach showed its effect in a confidence which the discouraged leader was already beginning to gain even before they actually talked over the problem. As they ate their lunch the education worker gave the discouraged worker ample opportunity to release his tension and get his troubles off his chest. This release seemed to be most helpful to the worker. There was something about the relationship between staff member and volunteer worker that helped. By the time the discouraged worker had told all of his woes and problems he himself began to see that things were not as bad as they had appeared.

After Mr. Sterling had told his story Wilson went back and asked for a re-evaluation on several points. After having done this, many of the points of contention which had been mentioned by Sterling did not seem to be as bad as they had the first time. This re-evaluation brought out some of the good sides of them as well. Then a fourth step which the education director used was to lead Mr. Sterling to take an inventory of the other responsibilities which he had in church life. When he saw that he was working in too many different areas, it was suggested by the education director that perhaps he needed to emphasize just a few areas of service and be able to do a more efficient job in them. When he was probed about his attitude toward the superintendency it became evident that Mr. Sterling surely didn't want to lose that, even though he was discouraged in it.

When Mr. Sterling became aware of the fact that he really wanted to keep the position, the education director came forth with another approach. This was to help him clarify his attitude toward his particular task in church life. Many times a person is unhappy in a particular situation because his attitude toward it is wrong. In other words, rather than changing the situation one must change his attitude. This is often true with an insoluble problem.

So after some discussion it was learned that many of the things which had caused the worker to be discouraged in this case were things that had to do with his attitude. Thus, the worker was able to lead Mr. Sterling into a sixth step in the process. It was to get the superintendent to discuss what might be causing his wrong attitude. He opened up the area of his fellow workers. Mr. Wilson was careful, however, not to lead him in the danger zone of reflecting any blame on them. The staff member was cautious not to sympathize with him to the extent of even allowing him to criticize his fellows. In so doing, the objections would lead to boosting the morale of the worker at the expense of the reputation of his fellow workers. Such a negative approach would never be advantageous.

As Mr. Wilson listened to the worker tell about his relationships to the fellow workers, it became rather obvious that his attitude was based on the fact that two of the teachers in his department seemed to be receiving much praise and compliment for their work. They were experienced teachers and their methods were attractive to their classes. It soon became evident that he was a little jealous of this attention and he felt that he was not doing a good enough job to get compliments.

Tactfully the educational man began to relate to him the various types of functions within a department. In doing so he skillfully and indirectly suggested that sometimes the best leaders are those who work behind the scenes. He mentioned the fact that this is always true of a superintendent who plans the programs and directs the committees. The education director, still talking in generalities, then went on to say that the superintendent's position was the most significant in the department. The teachers and committee members could not function without him. Then Mr. Wilson mentioned the successful assembly programs and good attendance campaigns Sterling had planned. By leading the worker to talk about his success, he led him to see for himself that he was really doing a good job.

After the two men had finished their lunch and were seated in the car, Mr. Wilson went into the deeper spiritual aspects of Christian service and in a brief prayer led the good superintendent to see that there were hidden satisfactions which were the real joys in church life.

It is evident from this typical case that a wise leader does not bring the discouraged worker out of his disappointment by simply slapping him on the back and telling him he is doing a good job. It requires some deeper process where the person is led to see the reason for his wrong attitude and his lack of faith.

## Our Independent Teen-agers

If the church worker would reach unenlisted teen-agers he must see them as normal persons passing through a phase of development intended by God. Adult leaders and parents should expect these healthy changes, not exaggerate them, and guide this development.

It is often said, "If you want to stay young, work with young people; if you want to die young, try to keep up with them." This is, of course, an extreme but typical idea about adolescents. We have been led to think that they are hard to reach and are going through an impossible period of development. This is not altogether true; we shall see that "helpfulness" is better than "amazement."

If you were to visit any typical library and go to the section of the stacks where books on adolescents and teen-agers are deposited, you would find one thing to be true with most of them. Most of the books emphasize the fact that teen-agers are supposed to be radically different. We have somehow slipped into this concept of adolescence and though we all agree there is rapid change and growth, we do not find this attitude of awe and amazement toward the changes that come in other ages.

For example, any Sunday school teacher or worker with young people can stand back and exclaim, "I just can't understand them," and try to relieve himself of the responsibility of his job. This will not reach them. He needs, rather, to get a new attitude which will cause him to look at the adolescent's needs and seek to help him meet them. When he seeks to help people on the basis of their needs, he *really* helps. Perhaps you are thinking now of Mary, a troubled young teen-ager in your group. If you knew something about her social life, her social relations, her childhood and her home life you could help her solve some of her problems. Anyone can aid a young person by looking at his life situations and needs. This is the first step in reaching them and is based on the fundamental viewpoint of helpfulness.

Young people can be reached when their process of development is accounted for. All steps in the human development process are necessary and important. When we see adolescence as a part of the total process, we see how normal it is. Some adults think, however, that young people are different because the changes come so rapidly at this time. They need to understand that this is one of the accelerated periods of change. The teen-ager is living with changes. Other people, who undergo major changes in later life, often have difficulties adjusting and we do not classify them as "different."

We have been influenced by the traditional attitudes which say, "The teen-ager is young, he's different, he's going through adolescence, and you can't reach him on any grounds." We will "wait until he gets over it" in our dealing with him. After all, we must remember that all people, young and old, must be dealt with individually. It is therefore grossly unfair for a Christian worker to not attempt to lead a person just because of the group to which he belongs.

Often young people are estranged and feel alone at this time. Therefore, it means that the adults who are leading them must give guidance and help — then they can be reached. Many young people are running away from life by not facing up to the choices which are essential to their maturity. Such avoidance is an unhealthy symptom in the life of any teen-ager. Teen-agers should be stepping out and making their decisions because they are anxious to become independent. This is true in life adjustment. They ought not to feel alone in this.

Church leaders will not always be able to reach young people. However, seeing their perspective always helps. This can be done by understanding the changes they face, being helpful during these changes, allowing for their expressions of independence, providing wholesome satisfactions for their growing needs, and constantly holding an attitude of helpfulness for them.

## The Single Adult

Never have single adults been more able to prepare for service to fellow men and to God as now. Do you know a man like Bill Williams? Bill is a single adult who, when he finished college, went into a small business. He is one of the most active men in the civic life of the community. He sponsors several youth groups and makes a contribution to the lives of the boys not only by his work but by his example. Bill could find a greater area of service in church than in any other place. Here he could place the emphasis of his life. Bill should be one of those valuable persons in the church who has the happy combination of both maturity and the enthusiasm of youth. He would be able to lead a group of young people in the church to come to the most dedicated and constructive level of Christian living that people have seen in a long time. In his position in life he has considerable time and also the ability to personally decide how he will use it. Because of this freedom he would be able to serve untiringly in the Lord's work.

Helen Thomas is typical of the many attractive single women bubbling over with enthusiasm and creative ideas. She has a sincere, mature, Christian faith. She not only holds a number of responsible positions in the church, but when there is a need for extra help in the office or for a pianist or chorister, she is the first one to respond. She is attractive to the children in the church and they all adore her; at the same time her maturity gives a feeling of confidence to the adults as she leads their children. She accepts this responsibility as one of stewardship under God.

The needs of single adults are those which are natural for any adults, but ones which are sometimes more intense. These needs often involve opportunities for personal expression and also for social contacts. The church can reach these single adults and provide an outlet for the satisfaction of these needs. We can see that there is the motivation to belong to the group.

Usually single adults fall into two categories with reference to loyalty to the church. The one group includes those who completely estrange themselves from the church, having left it in their intermediate days and often returning in middle adult life. The other group constitutes the young single adults who have remained true to Christ during this period of life and usually assume leadership positions in the church. Many times those who have separated themselves from the church are simply seeking, in groups outside the church, to satisfy their social needs.

Single adults, because of their educational, vocational and social development, are usually creative and enthusiastic. Thus, they can serve the church in outstanding ways — particularly in programing. Many of them are in vocational or professional work which definitely relates to church activities. There can often be a wonderful carry-over from the secular work to church work.

The story is told about a single woman who was the counselor for the high school in a small city. She had extensive training in the field of counseling and guidance and really was the only person in the town who was so qualified. Her services to the church in counseling with young people would be invaluable. She was approached about work in the church as a counselor and her acceptance began a profitable experience for all those involved.

In another church a single man had been an outstanding sales representative in the community for a number of years. He was, however, irregular in church attendance and interest. When the church launched its building program, this single adult man was made chairman of the money raising campaign. His genuine enthusiasm and knowledge of the field of selling were used in a remarkable way by the Lord. His enthusiasm and ability to devote unending hours of time to the project were rewarded by the church's oversubscripting its goal.

One could think of many other examples of church situations in which young single adults have made unusual and peculiar contributions. A number of years ago I made a survey of the young people, single and married, in the state of Missouri as to their service in local churches. In this study it was found that a high percentage of the real leadership in organizational church life constituted this group of single adults.

The average adult who is single and in a career or business is so creative and enthusiastic that his abilities need expression. It is tragic when this expression is given to causes less worthy than that of the church. Here is the church's opportunity.

Single adults also need the kind of spiritual fellowship a local church provides. Christ intended that this social unit be supplemented by the contributions of families of the church. In time of lonesomeness and crisis a church family can prove invaluable to such a single adult.

The membership of the church should see to it that single adults are frequently invited into the homes of church members who are married. What better way to reach them for Christian service?

## Our Aging Senior Citizens

"How do you feel about approaching old age? What are you doing to prepare for it? What part can the church play in the later years of your life? Do you think many people take into consideration the place of spiritual security and of Christian friends?" Every Christian leader ought to ask himself questions like these if he would understand and reach older people.

Only as one sees the total sweep of this life, change by change, will he be ready to understand the "golden years" successfully.

In his book, *Making the Most of the Rest of Life,* Dr. Karl Stolz says that adulthood is divided into four periods. They are adjustment: twenty-five to the thirty-fifth year; achievement: thirty-five to fifty-five; conservation: fifty-five to sixty-five; and retirement: sixty-five and up.[1] These terms "conservation" and "retirement" are good keys to reaching mature adults. In conservation (working diligently to save) the adult must be reached at the point of needing spiritual conservation also. In retirement, church activities must be provided.

*Attitudes for retirement are important.* Many older people are in the category of two mature adults who were discussing their coming retirement. The younger of the

[1]Karl Stolz, *Making the Most of the Rest of Life* (New York: Abingdon-Cokesbury, 1941).

two asked his friend, who was beginning retirement, what he planned to do the first year. The older man answered that he was going to get a rocking chair and put it on the front porch.

Then the younger asked, "What are your plans for the second year?"

The older man answered, "Then I'll start rocking."

This attitude of inactivity in retirement is typical. Retired people are reached by church leaders who show them the opportunities of church activity. Enjoyable activities ought to be planned which carry out the viewpoint that retirement is an active experience.

A part of the problem is, of course, financial. Therefore, financial preparation is important. However, the right attitude toward money in retirement is more important than the money itself. Aging people can participate in church life without financial obligation. Basic security comes from the spiritual resources which are explained and enhanced by the leadership of the church.

*The value of interests for retirement.* The older church member who is hard to reach must be led to see the part a church can play in his retirement interests. Some qualifications which make retirement interests good resources are as follows:

A retirement activity must be creative and productive. For example, fishing as a sport might not suffice psychologically. However, if some of the fish caught were sold for income, this retirement activity might work. Just so, all church interests should be creative and productive.

Retirement activities must be personally satisfying. This means that friendships are essential. The church group provides such fellowship. Life in retirement must have a focal point of love and interest. Life in the later years needs to be "living that is goalward." The writer of Proverbs said, "The fear of the Lord prolongeth days" (Proverbs 10:27). Therefore, these goals ought to be of a spiritual nature and achieved along with Christian friends. One feels sorry for a young person who does not know friends with the same life goals, but he pities even more the older person in this circumstance.

People in the church can provide the right kind of friendships and the proper atmosphere. One of the nation's leading authorities on retirement has, in his popular book in the field, suggested that a church provides the best social atmosphere for a couple during the later years. In a recent newspaper article, the chairman of the United States committee on the aging reported a list of the places in which people in retirement can find friends. He told where they can best seek them out. Churches are number one on his list. Selling the aged on this point is one of the best enlistment approaches for them.

*The aged are hungry for security.* Spiritual security is the most necessary thing in the world, especially to an older person. Many retired people seek to find security outside of the church. Aged people tend to need the confidence which the church members can give them. The feeling of fellowship with other older Christians is more significant than food and water.

Our senior citizens are easier to reach when we know their physical, social and spiritual needs better.

All of these who are difficult to enlist usually respond to the method of suggestion. In the earlier discussion on indirect methods in Chapter Five, there are helps which apply to the particular cases of the present chapter. In summary, however, there are about five ways to use suggestion with those who are hard to reach.

One — be subtle in your approaches. As indicated before, this must be clearly differentiated from being tricky or ensnaring in one's attitude.

Two — emphasize the thing which you desire the person to do, and give as little criticism of his present pattern of behavior as possible. One must remember that many of these who are hard to reach are sensitive about their present condition. From the standpoint of the Christian zeal and urgency, one cannot overdo this point but rather must find a happy medium.

Three — infer the desired outcome as seen by the church leader. This means that inference becomes one of the best tools to use with the hard to reach. If this method is used it gives more freedom to the person in choosing his own way, whereas, if the church leader comes to him with too obvious a plan of attack, it seems as though the person being reached is being directed too much. This is particularly true in dealing with the prominent and the wealthy. It has particular application with the discouraged and the single adult also.

Four — infer the answer you want by the type of questioning used. For example, negative, "You don't want to . . . do you?" or positive, "you want to . . . don't you?" We often think of this conditioning of answers as a good method to use in religious education with children and we forget that it is an excellent method to use with many other age groups as well. This is particularly true in dealing with the teen-ager and the timid or lonesome person.

Five — it may require repeated and consistent impressions which are still suggestive but which make an impact. This, again, is particularly helpful in reaching the self-centered person, the timid one, the single adult and the aged person. We are all familiar with the use of repetition on the television commercial, but it is too obvious and directive here. This more subtle approach is a constant impression of the idea we are trying to get across, but without so much force and coercion.

In conclusion, there is one warning remark that needs to be made, and that is, with some people who are hard to reach — particularly the prominent and the wealthy — it is best to not use suggestion but to openly reach the appeal and be frank with the individual. It will be remembered that Christ frequently used this approach with prominent people and it was effective. As mentioned earlier, some of the people in places of influence are so skilled in human relations that they see through our indirect and suggestion methods and really respond better to a direct approach.

# 9. WHEN TECHNIQUES FAIL

# WHEN TECHNIQUES FAIL

THE RIGHT KINDS OF FRIENDSHIPS MUST BE CULTIVATED
CHRISTIAN FRIENDSHIPS ARE BUILT ON CHRISTIAN LOVE
"I AM A PRODUCT OF ALL WHOM I HAVE MET"
FAILURE NECESSITATES MORE SACRIFICE

## Chapter Nine

## WHEN TECHNIQUES FAIL

We have looked at some of the methods of human relations as developed by men. Most of them have been tried and proven by psychologists. Others are the results of personal trial and error testing. Some are the formulation of "common-sense" judgments of human nature. Most of the time, if people and situations are more or less typical, they will operate successfully. God uses these methods as He leads *through people.* Christian workers are responsible for employing every legitimate and tactful tool possible, under God, as they work with people.

However, when these techniques fail the Christian leader must still work. What does he do? First, he relies on more prayer. God *can enable* him to do that which he did not accomplish, if it is in God's will. Also, the leader bolsters himself with an increased faith and rededication. Frequently he places more emphasis on friendship, love, self evaluation and personal improvement. He may see that he needs to be more sacrificial. He has done these things all along, but failure may indicate a need for increase.

Now we are going to look at some ways to cultivate friends, some characteristics of the love which bind Christian friends together, the product of friendships in life, and what friendships will cost us in the position of leadership.

### THE RIGHT KINDS OF FRIENDSHIPS MUST BE CULTIVATED

Mrs. Glenn Young, a Sunday school teacher in Centerville, was always disgruntled because she had no friends. Finally she talked with her pastor about the situation and he suggested some means of cultivating friends. He assured her that she had an attractive personality, a fine home and a respected husband, but he led her to see that she had been waiting for people to come to her and make her friendship. She needed to get out of her house, become more active in the church, and have people into her home socially. Soon Mrs. Young learned that for most people friends must be cultivated.

Some people find this an easy thing to do; others have some difficulty, but all must pay the price for having friends. Even Jesus went out to where the people were. Paul traveled most of the known world and we, too, must usually take the initiative. Even if we are the type of people to whom others are naturally attracted, we will soon lose their friendship if we do not return that true friendship in deeds and love. We cannot depend on methods only. We can observe that attractive people who do not return the friendship of all of their following have a constantly changing circle of friends.

Then finally, it pays to develop the right kinds of friends — Christian friends who will stimulate us to higher living. For example, frequently a young married couple has been led down because of friends with low standards. How many of our parents met each other in a church group and courted in that group? They were then married in that church and continued to grow and mature in the church family. Are our children as fortunate now? To a degree, you can determine whom your children will marry and the kind of homes they will have. You can do it by helping them cultivate the right circle of friends.

## Christian Friendships Are Built on Christian Love

Have you met some greedy people who wanted to make many friends just for the sake of being popular? Some people gather friends as they do stamps or butterflies to be added to a collection. These people are cheap "politicians." It is good for one to have many friends if each is held in high personal respect and love. Great Christians can be acquainted with many people, but their friendships never become "mass production." Jesus spoke to multitudes, but His message was couched in such personal love that each listener felt that the Lord was interested in him as an individual. Neither love nor religion can be real and vital if not personal. What are some characteristics of this love that makes friendships real?

*Love may begin as a one way thing; but true love and friendship look forward to fulfillment in a two way exchange.* The Bible says that God first loved us and the process is not complete until we return that love. You first love an unsaved person enough to tell him about Christ, but after he becomes a Christian your friendship is at its richest. A one way friendship ought not to go on forever.

A Christian leader must both love and be lovable. His colleagues and followers accept his leadership when it is cased in a two-way relationship of sincere, brotherly love.

*Love can't be coerced.* Even as one patiently leads people to love the Lord, he so encourages devotion. A "forced" love is a dead love. You can't demand that people love you. You can't force lost people to love Christ. You must build love by feeding it regularly.

*Expressing love.* If our loving attitude is consistently expressed in deeds, as we deal with people, we can lead them. Even as our personal love to Christ must be shown in church attendance and daily prayer, even as a plant must be regularly fed, so must our loving attitudes toward people be consistent!

*Making our love for others personal as we deal with them.* "Mass production love" means nothing; one must show others that he is intimately concerned about every issue in the person's life.

*Feeding other lives.* When you meet the real needs of people's lives, they will love you!

Keep reminding yourself of your love of individuals. Do not let it be taken for granted and become mechanical in your contacts. The leader of a group ought to enter each session with a renewed love and concern for the members as persons — if he doesn't, they can tell it. This will work when fixed methods will not.

## "I Am a Product of All Whom I Have Met"

Tennyson spoke these well-known words. Next to the experience of conversion in Christ, one's personality is changed most by the kinds of friends he has. The people with whom one associates daily modify his life as he is changing their lives by his contact with them. ". . . and they took knowledge of them, that they had been with Jesus" (Acts 4:13b). Many criminals have walked the road of sin paved with the wrong kinds of friends. Every saint has been brought closer to God by good friendships through the years. Something in leaders' lives "rubs off" on people when they associate with leaders who are stimulating and honorable. One's moral life is greatly conditioned by his leaders who are true friends.

Therefore, the church leader can use the influence of his friendship to guide people when his learned methods do not meet the need.

## Failure Necessitates More Sacrifice

When techniques have failed it may mean that in addition to reliance upon friendship and love one must also train himself better so as to be more capable of the use of good methods in the future. He must face up to the additional sacrifices in his leadership role. The price of leadership is a high one. God greatly rewards, but He expects sacrificial living by those who serve Him.

Some of the prices of true leadership for the Christian worker are these:

*Faithfulness to the end.* Many times the church worker fails because he has not been patient enough to enable his faith to carry on when his methods do not succeed. This is the opposite of the case of the democratic Christian leader of great faith who labors on beyond technical methods and relies upon his belief in God and his confidence in his task. It relates to his "sense of mission." The Christian leader keeps on keeping on to the end. Finally, if this strong faith persists, he will usually succeed in his human relationships.

*Another price is long hours of study and preparation.* This refers to both his personal spiritual life in devotional preparation and also further planning and self improvement. It also involves his becoming more and more sensitive to details. In this entire study of the psychology of church leadership it has been evident that the Christian worker must be sensitive to the responses of those whom he leads. This is an expensive price to pay. It is easier to hasten through life and avoid these details.

*There are elements of self-denial.* This means long hours and many times the sacrifice of time usually given to recreation and social pleasures. The leader must be willing to pay the price of time and energy in order to do God's work successfully.

*It will occasionally cost the price of offending someone.* Every leader who is successful has had to pay this price at one time or another. It is difficult for the Christian leader to take the long look, yet circumstances sometimes come to the point where one must take the welfare of the group as his rule. In so doing he may have to offend a minority group or an individual. The Christian worker doesn't want to do this, but even our Saviour found times when it was expedient to the larger evangelistic and missionary cause.

*One of the heaviest burdens of the Christian leader is that of his responsibility.* No one likes to assume the responsibility of other people's lives, yet the Christian leader is compelled to do so. There are times — though he avoids them — when he must advise. Shouldering the fact that many people depend upon him for moral and spiritual guidance is a heavy weight. Then, there is always the possibility of his leading the people in the wrong way, for he is human and will make some mistakes. All of these can cause the leader to have many moments of discouragement and depression. If he has the greater Cause on his heart, he will be willing to pay this price also.

*A great price is that of keeping confidences.* No one can lead people in a successful way who cannot keep the confidences of his colleagues and followers. For some leaders this is more difficult than for others — but it is essential for all. As long as we are working with human beings this becomes one of the necessities of our task.

*Perhaps the highest price which the leader pays is that of lonesomeness.* This means that the more democratic the leader is, the more he will have to face up to this fact. The leader must spend many hours in prayer and personal preparation. He must often lead in a way that he feels is best, but which is not pleasing at all. This alone has the element of lonesomeness involved in it. In addition to this there will be times when the people turn against his wishes and he is forced to change his plans. He may feel extremely lonely at these times.

And so sacrifices are part of serving the Lord and all must meet the test. When our human approaches do not work it may mean that we must give more of ourselves in order to succeed in a task to which we have been called. But we have, in the fellowship of Christ and in the divine guidance of the Holy Word, that which we need to succeed. In Christ all things are possible. "Jesus said unto him, If thou canst believe, all things are possible to him that believeth" (Mark 9:23).

"If you were to take the sum total of all the authoritative articles ever written by the most qualified of psychologists and psychiatrists on the subject of mental hygiene, if you were to combine them and refine them and cleave out the excess verbage, if you were to take the whole of the meat and none of the parsley, and if you were to have these unadulterated bits of pure scientific knowledge concisely expressed by the most capable of living poets, you would have an awkward and incomplete summation of the Sermon on the Mount."[1]

Modern psychology and the laws of interpersonal relations will never take the place of simple Christian love. Our leaders and workers need a healthy combination of both to bring imperfect, sinful human beings to a divine relationship with God.

---

[1]James T. Fisher and Lowell S. Hawley, A Few Buttons Missing, The Case Book of a Psychiatrist (J. B. Lippincott Co.: Philadelphia and New York, 1951), p. 273.

BIBLIOGRAPHY

# BIBLIOGRAPHY (for additional study)

Ackland, Donald F., *Joy in Church Membership* (Nashville: Convention Press), 1955.

Banks, Murray, *How to Live with Yourself* (New York: Prentice Hall), 1951.

Barnette, Jasper Newton, *A Church Using Its Sunday School* (rev. ed.) (Nashville: Convention Press), 1951.

————, *The Pull of the People* (revised) (Nashville: Convention Press), 1956.

Bettger, Frank, *How I Raised Myself from Failure to Success in Selling* (first edition) (New York: Prentice Hall), 1949.

Britt, Steuart Henderson, *Social Psychology of Modern Life* (New York: Rinehart and Co., Inc.), 1941.

Burkhalter, Frank Elisha, *Living Abundantly* (Nashville: Sunday School Board of the Southern Baptist Convention), 1942.

Campbell, Doak S., *When Do Teachers Teach?* (Nashville: Sunday School Board of the Southern Baptist Convention), 1935.

Carnegie, Dale, *How to Stop Worrying and Start Living* (New York: Simon and Schuster), 1948. (New York: Pocket Books), 1953.

————, *How to Win Friends and Influence People* (New York: Pocket Books), 1940.

Corzine, J. L., *Looking at Learning* (Nashville: Sunday School Board of the Southern Baptist Convention), 1934.

————, *Teaching to Win and Develop* (Nashville: Sunday School Board of the Southern Baptist Convention), 1954.

DeSchweinitz, Karl, *The Art of Helping People Out of Trouble* (Boston and New York: Houghton, Mifflin Co.), 1924.

Dobbins, Gaines Stanley, *A Winning Witness* (Nashville: Sunday School Board of the Southern Baptist Convention), 1938.

————, *Deepening the Spiritual Life* (rev. ed.) (Nashville: Sunday School Board of the Southern Baptist Convention), 1954.

————, *Meeting the Needs of Adults Through the Baptist Training Union* (Nashville: Sunday School Board of the Southern Baptist Convention), 1949.

————, *Working Together in a Spiritual Democracy* (Nashville: Sunday School Board of the Southern Baptist Convention), 1935.

Edsall, Florence S., *Success and What It Takes* (New York: Morrow), 1954.

157

Flake, Arthur, *Building a Standard Sunday School* (rev. ed.) (Nashville: Convention Press), 1954.

Fosdick, Harry Emerson, *On Being a Real Person* (New York: Harper and Brothers), 1943.

Gibson, James B., *Growing Younger Through Friendship* (New York: Vantage Press), 1952.

Gordon, Julius, *Your Sense of Humor* (New York: Didier), 1950.

Gray, John Stanley, *Psychology Applied to Human Affairs* (second edition) (New York: McGraw-Hill), 1954.

Guntrip, Henry James Samuel, *Psychology for Ministers and Social Workers* (London: Independent Press), 1949.

Hepner, Harry Walker, *Psychology Applied to Life and Work* (Madison, Wisconsin: Published for the U. S. Armed Force Institute), 1956.

Hickman, Frank S., *Possible Self* (New York: Abingdon), 1933.

Hopkins, Granville Shelby, *Tomorrow You Lead* (rev. ed.) (Nashville: Sunday School Board of the Southern Baptist Convention), 1954.

Hovland, Carl Iver, *Communication and Persuasion* (New Haven: Yale University Press), 1953.

Hudson, R. Lofton, *Growing a Christian Personality* (Nashville: Sunday School Board of the Southern Baptist Convention), 1955.

Husband, Richard W., *Applied Psychology* (New York: Harper and Brothers), 1949.

Ingram, Karl Culton, *Winning Your Way with People* (New York: Whittlesey House), 1949.

Kahm, Harold S., *You Can Be Successful and Follow the Golden Rule* (New York: Wilcox and Follett Co.), 1947.

Laird, Donald Anderson, *Increasing Personal Efficiency* (third edition) (New York: Harper and Brothers), 1936.

————, *Sizing Up People* (New York: McGraw-Hill), 1951.

————, *The Technique of Building Personal Leadership* (New York: McGraw-Hill), 1946.

Lambdin, J. E., *Building a Church Training Program* (Nashville: Sunday School Board of the Southern Baptist Convention), 1952.

Lindgren, Henry Clay, *The Art of Human Relations* (first edition) (New York: Hermitage House), 1953.

————, *Effective Leadership in Human Relations* (first edition) (New York: Hermitage House), 1954.

Maier, Norman R. F., *Principles of Human Relations* (New York: John Wiley and Sons), 1952.

Matthews, Charles Evert, *Every Christian's Job* (Nashville: Broadman Press), 1951.

Price, J. M., *Formative Factors in Christian Character* (Nashville: Sunday School Board of the Southern Baptist Convention), 1959.

————, *Mastering Life's Problems* (Nashville: Convention Press), 1958.

Reilly, William John, *Successful Human Relations: Principles and Practice in Business, in the Home, in Government* (first edition) (New York: Harper), 1952.

Remmers, Herman Henry, *Introduction to Opinion and Attitude Measurement* (New York: Harper), 1954.

Rigell, William R., *Investments in Christian Living* (Nashville: Convention Press), 1930.

Sanderson, Leonard, *Personal Soul-Winning* (Nashville: Sunday School Board of the Southern Baptist Convention), 1958.

————, *Using the Sunday School in Evangelism* (Nashville: Sunday School Board of the Southern Baptist Convention), 1958.

Sartre, Jean Paul, *The Psychology of Imagination* (London: Rider and Co.), 1950.

Schmidt, Warren H., *Techniques That Produce Teamwork* (New London, Conn.: A. C. Croft Publications), 1954.

Sidis, Boris, *The Psychology of Suggestion* (New York: D. Appleton and Co.), 1919.

Sisemore, John T., *The Ministry of Visitation* (Nashville: Broadman Press), 1954.

Thomason, Calvin Cornelius, *Human Relations in Action* (second edition) (New York: Prentice Hall), 1954.

Titus, Charles Hickman, *The Processes of Leadership* (Dubuque, Iowa: W. C. Brown Co.), 1950.

Uris, Auren, *How to Be a Successful Leader* (New York: McGraw-Hill), 1953.

Van Ness, Isaac J., *Training in Church Membership* (Nashville: Sunday School Board of the Southern Baptist Convention), 1908.

Watts, Joseph Thomas, *The Growing Christian* (Nashville: Sunday School Board of the Southern Baptist Convention), 1937.

Wetherill, Richard W., *The Dynamics of Human Relations* (New York: D. Van Nostrand Co.), 1949.

Wheeler, Elmer, *How to Sell Yourself to Others* (first edition) (New York: Macmillan), 1941.

Wright, Milton, *Getting Along with People* (New York, London: Whittlesey House, McGraw-Hill Book Co.), 1935.